Praise for *Educational Research*

Here's a must for the staff library; useful for any staff thinking of taking a higher degree – and there are many – and vital to a school keen on using research findings and in setting out to base their improvement on practical school-based research.

Sir Tim Brighouse, former London Schools Commissioner and
Chief Education Officer for Birmingham and Oxfordshire

In capturing an education zeitgeist, this book provides teachers with a thoroughly engaging, much needed introductory guide to refer to when engaging with education research. I particularly like the fact that ethical issues are given precedence right at the beginning of the book. As the authors say, all too often ethical considerations can be given scant regard or seen as a procedural, box ticking exercise when conducting research. Yet by foregrounding its importance, Phil and Joan are developing a crucial, ethical awareness in the reader from the outset of the book. Practising what they preach and starting as they mean to go on! This is a book well worth reading for any teacher thinking about dipping their toe in the education research waters or even those who simply want to find out more about the subject.

Dr Matt O'Leary, Reader in Education, Centre for the Study of Practice
and Culture in Education (CSPACE), Birmingham City University

Educational Research provides an engaging insight into research principles, methods and frameworks. Every step of the research process is clearly presented: from the design of surveys and questionnaires and getting the most out of interviews, all the way to thinking about how best to analyse and present your data.

Importantly, Wood and Smith have placed ethics at the heart of this book. The principles of honesty, transparency and care underpin every stage of the research process as they describe it. Crafting any educational research project using *Educational Research* will set you on the path to results that are credible, fairer and more robust.

So, this book is a goldmine for any teacher who regularly asks themselves, 'What changes do I want or need to see?', 'How will I bring these about?' and 'What will I try then?' The delight of this book is that it also gives us an answer to the final impact question, '…and how will I truly know it's made a difference?' Packed with practical tools, examples and reflective questions, *Educational Research* will add to and expand the research repertoire of every classroom teacher.

So simply open up the first page and get started.

Zoë Elder, Executive Director, Clevedon Learning Hub,
independent education consultant, author of *Full On Learning*

This book is well-structured and considers all the main points first-time research-ers need to consider. The examples are particularly beneficial for students studying short research modules, as seen on our PGCE course, and the section on ethics provides simple, clear explanations of the important aspects to consider. I would certainly recommend this to students I am teaching and supervising as an acces-sible introduction into this aspect of academic writing.

Jenny Fogarty, Senior Lecturer, Division of Education,
London South Bank University

Phil Wood and Joan Smith have written a neat guide to educational research which will contribute nicely to the burgeoning research-in-education business. Wood and Smith demonstrate with utter clarity that undertaking your own research is a complicated business. What I like most is their acknowledgement that educational research should 'always be understood and utilised through the filter of professional values and judgement'. *Educational Research* explains the nuances of research and will prove an invaluable guide for anyone on the verge of engaging in developing an evidence-informed approach to teaching.

John Tomsett, Head Teacher, Huntington School, York

Educational Research summarises all the areas for a new researcher to consider. It is a very accessible resource, not only because of the way it is written but also because of the examples and case studies which the authors provide. These show the complexity and also the rewards of undertaking research. Particularly helpful are the summaries of other key books on research.

Mary Myatt, school adviser and blogger marymyatt.com

Following a 30-year career as an educational practitioner, I embarked on a profes-sional doctorate in 2010. I really wish this book had been available then! It is a comprehensive, clear and accessible guide to how to conduct research, particularly single, small-scale projects, in a responsible and rigorous way.

The readable style and accessible language reflect the book's intended audience of professionals, rather than the academic community. The key message is communi-cated in a compelling way – the importance of being 'positively critical', of avoiding bias and ensuring ethical principles underpin all stages of the research process. Wood and Smith argue convincingly that the best way to develop research literacy is to conduct your own research. This book will help you to do so in a way which is informed and robust. My only complaint is the timing of the publication of the book – just as I submit my doctoral thesis …

Jill Berry, former head teacher, educational consultant and researcher

Educational Research
Taking the Plunge

Phil Wood and Joan Smith

 Independent Thinking Press

First published by

Independent Thinking Press
Crown Buildings, Bancyfelin, Carmarthen,
Wales, SA33 5ND, UK
www.independentthinkingpress.com

Independent Thinking Press is an imprint of Crown House Publishing Ltd.

British Library Cataloguing-in-Publication Data
A catalogue entry for this book is available from the British Library.

Print ISBN 978-1-78135-240-3
Mobi ISBN 978-1-78135-249-6
ePub ISBN 978-1-78135-250-2
ePDF ISBN 978-1-78135-251-9

Printed and bound in the UK by
TJ International, Padstow, Cornwall

In memory of Kathleen Smith
(1926–2015).

Contents

1. **What is research?** **1**

Introduction 1

What are some of the foundations of good educational research? 2

The interdisciplinary nature of educational research 7

Becoming research literate 8

Introduction to the remaining chapters 10

2. **Ethical issues in educational research** **13**

Introduction 13

Basic principles of ethical research 14

    Consent 14

    Honesty 17

    Care 20

Managing researcher bias 24

    Managing researcher bias in the research design 25

    Managing researcher bias in data collection 26

    Managing researcher bias in organising and analysing data 27

    Managing researcher bias in reporting findings 29

Summary 31

3. **Critical reading and writing** **33**

Introduction 33

What do we mean by 'criticality'? 33

Critical thinking, writing and friendship 34

Critical reading and writing in your research 36

Theoretical framework 39

Discussion and analysis of findings 41

Writing clearly and critically 42

    Avoid jargon and convoluted language 43

    Check your grammar 44

    Make sure each paragraph communicates a key point 45

    Match subheadings to content 46

    Eliminate overstatement and redundant phrases 46

    Be your own editor 47

Summary 48

4.   **Thinking about the basics** **49**

Introduction 49

Interests 49

Context 52

Research questions 53

Summary 58

5.   **Worldviews and methodologies** **59**

Introduction 59

Grappling with the philosophy of research 59

    Ontology 60

    Epistemology 62

    Worldviews 62

Methodologies 64

    Action research 64

    Surveys 69

    Case studies 72

    Experimental methodologies 76

    Mixed methods 79

Summary 83

6.   **Considering data capture** **85**

Introduction 85

Sampling 85

    Probability sampling 87

    Nonprobability sampling 88

Data collection 89

    Questionnaires 90

    Interviews 96

    Observations 99

    Visual methods 102

Summary 105

7.   **Thinking about data** **107**

Introduction 107

Validity and reliability 107

Analysing data 110

Quantitative data analysis 111

    Types of quantitative data 111

    Worked example of some basic descriptive statistics 114

Qualitative data analysis 120

    Extract from interview with Coral 125

Summary 129

8.   **Developing small-scale research** **131**

Introduction 131

Summary 137

Appendix 1: Developing your understanding of research methods –
*   suggested further reading* 139

Appendix 2: Exemplar research ethics consent form 143

References 145

Index 147

Chapter 1
What is research?

Introduction

Since 2010 there has been an increasingly wide interest in the role of research in education, particularly in schools. Initially this interest tended to emphasise the idea of uncovering 'what works' in classrooms. Such an approach is not surprising as there is a ready appeal in seeing research as a medium for 'solving' issues in schools, and particularly in classrooms. The impression can be given that research will ultimately lead to a recipe book from which we can find the 'correct' ways to teach or ensure good behaviour in lessons. However, research is a complex process which can be approached in many different ways to offer insights into a very wide range of questions. We argue that research can play an important role in offering ideas and insights into educational issues, but it should always be understood and utilised through the filter of professional values and judgement; it should never be seen as a recipe book to be slavishly followed.

In 1983, Donald Schon wrote *The Reflective Practitioner*, which was an argument for positioning reflective practice at the centre of teacher work. He identified two forms of reflection:

- *Reflection in action*: The ability we develop within our own practice which focuses on our constant assessment about what we're doing as we do it. When we assess that something is not working, we use our experience and knowledge to alter activity in the moment. This often occurs when something out of the ordinary happens, giving us a reason to alter our practice as the event or activity unfolds.

- *Reflection on action*: This is based on describing, analysing, reviewing and evaluating practice beyond the immediacy of the classroom to gain a deeper understanding of our work, particularly to help identify areas for improvement in the future.

Reflective practice has become an important activity which teachers are expected to undertake to improve their pedagogy. Whilst valuable, these activities predominantly rely on individual perception. There is little to ensure that what we think is an answer to our developmental needs is indeed as we see it, as our own biases and perceptions can give us a very partial view of the challenge or issue we are facing. If we decide we want to gain more structured, and possibly less biased, insights from our reflections as a way of interrogating our own perceptions, or if we want to engage with evidence from beyond our immediate classroom experience, then we are beginning to move from a reflective process to one of research.

In writing this book, we have two main aims in mind:

1. To introduce some of the basic concepts and knowledge underlying an understanding of research. This is important as research has a specialist language all of its own. To engage with and critique research we need to be able to understand how and why a piece of research has been developed in the way it has.

2. To provide some basic frameworks for developing your own small-scale research projects. As we will demonstrate later in this chapter, we believe that one of the best ways to deepen your understanding of research is to carry out your own!

We will therefore blend together discussion of some of the main concepts and knowledge concerning educational research with some basic frameworks and approaches for completing your own projects.

What are some of the foundations of good educational research?

If research is not synonymous with professional reflection, we need to try to define what it is and what some of the basic features of good research might be. There is no single, accepted definition of research across all subjects (more on that later), and even within education there are a large number of different approaches and traditions which understand research in different ways. Below we offer a definition merely as a starting point to aid discussion of what good research might include:

> The systematic investigation into, and study of, materials, sources, situations and people in order to explore and understand identified issues with the aim of reaching new insights.

This definition highlights the central notion that all research should be, in some way, systematic. But what do we mean by 'systematic'? We take this to mean that the work being undertaken has included some form of thoughtful planning, orientated around a clear focus and with a logical set of activities planned out to capture 'data'. The research activities which are developed will vary widely depending on the focus of the research. One researcher might be interested in a historic question which requires a lot of work with documents, whilst another may be interested in classroom practice requiring very different, and perhaps multiple, tools. Each research project requires careful consideration of how and why data are collected, and the underlying assumptions on which the research is based.

Research is about exploring and understanding issues. As such, it should not be seen as a linear endeavour that automatically provides continuous improvements to practice. Research can lead to results which are unexpected (often seen as 'negative') or find little evidence of change or improvement. In either case, the research should not be seen as a failure; all insights are important, and frequently it is research which turns out to be counter-intuitive that leads to new, interesting questions and foci for further work. To ensure we don't attempt to second-guess and produce insights which fit with our preconceptions, we need to develop logical and carefully considered approaches to research – approaches which we will eventually share transparently with others. The full disclosure of our research approaches when reporting is crucial so that readers can fairly critique and engage with our work. Much of the research in education will add to our understanding of practical issues, but rarely, if ever, will it give us absolute truths or laws. This is why we suggest that research can help us to gain new insights, but it rarely leads to solid, universal conclusions.

From this consideration of the nature of research, we will outline what we think are the features of good research in education. These principles underlie our discussion of research methods throughout this book:

- *Focuses on a definable issue or problem.* Research needs to be focused on a clear area for exploration. If it is too broad it becomes unwieldy which makes it difficult to collect meaningful data. In attempting to develop a coherent focus for research, the appropriate use of research questions is extremely important.

- *Emphasises an ethical approach.* All research in education should be developed with the explicit understanding that it should be an ethical process. The vast majority of research in this field includes human participants in some way. Our research should always protect the well-being and dignity of both participants and researchers. This is often the stated purpose of research ethics, the 'legal' aspects of which are the primary focus of review panels. However, we stress that ethical research should also focus on the need for honest and transparent reporting so that work can be read critically and fairly by peers. This includes the reporting of research approaches, any conflicts of interest and the context of the research. It also requires that when we rely on the work of others, we reference them fully so that they are given due recognition for their work.

- *Gives a clear outline of the context of research.* The process of education is highly complex. Therefore, when writing about research it is always important to give readers a clear context (albeit anonymised). If a small-scale study is completed with a class of 12- and 13-year-olds in an inner-city school composed predominantly of more able students, then it is essential that the reader has this information so they can understand the context of the data gained. This also allows the reader to consider the degree of relevance of the research to their own situation. It is a central part of honest and transparent reporting and educational debate.

- *Uses research literature to inform the research design.* The vast majority of research builds on work already done. It is important to begin to gain an understanding of the research which has been published previously in an area of interest. We need to be good at reading and assessing research so that we can judge the degree of evidence on which we might build our own work.

- *Gives a clear outline/discussion of the methodology and methods which have been used to collect data.* Ethical research should make the methodology and methods which have been used to collect data transparent. Readers need to know how our research has been carried out as this is crucial to being able to interpret the data, and therefore engage critically with any claims that are made. By explaining decisions concerning preferred methodologies we give an insight into the way the research is positioned and the nature of the claims made.

An account of the data collection tools (methods) used is equally important for the same reasons. If a study has used interviews, are the questions reported so that we can judge the level of neutrality? Where observations are used, is the focus and method of data capture explained? If these issues are not thought through and reported then a considered, critical reading of the research cannot be achieved.

Where research occurs at a meta-level – for example, through the use of literature reviews – it should include a methodology outlining the search criteria, filtering processes and how publications have been analysed. If a literature review merely presents an area of research with no methodology, it needs to be read with caution as we have no way of assessing its validity.

- *Uses appropriate methods which clearly link back to the initial issues/ problems and research questions.* Well-conceived research will be able to make clear how particular methods help in investigating the chosen issues/research questions; this gives the research coherence.

- *Analyses collected data in a transparent way.* In the same way as it is important to carefully consider the reporting of methodology and methods, so it is with analysing the data which have been collected. Analysis is often not considered to the same level of detail as methodology and data collection, but it is crucial in ensuring a reasoned and valid consideration of the data, particularly when trying to minimise biases and the selective use of data. To make the process transparent, it is again important to report how data have been analysed.

- *Develops explanations and discussion derived from the data.* Good research develops a clear discussion of the data collected. This is at the centre of reporting research, in the same way as it is when the interpretation of the project is developed. It is crucial that explanations emerge from the data provided and are not dissonant with the evidence. In addition, the discussion of the data should be related to the literature with which you have engaged and which is the foundation on which the research study rests.

- *Offers measured insights/conclusions.* Good research is measured in the claims made. Small-scale research cannot easily make claims which can be scaled up; in other words, an analysis of one cycle of action research focusing on, for example, improving questioning practices in one class, cannot act as the basis for national policy. However, small-scale research can still provide valuable insights for practitioners by providing useful information as to where good practice might be found. Within large-scale research, projects often rely on quantitative analyses. Insights here tend to be based on statistical manipulations which offer a constructive exploration of patterns and trends. However, in-depth explanations are sometimes more problematic as this type of research is more likely to provide answers to the 'what' rather than the 'why'.

All research has potential shortcomings because no approach is perfect or has all of the answers in a particular area of interest. Often, deep insights occur through the long-term application of a number of qualitative and quantitative approaches which augment understanding and give progressively fuller and more critical perspectives on an issue.

The interdisciplinary nature of educational research

Many academic disciplines have a generally well-understood and accepted philosophical approach to investigation and knowledge generation. As a result, they do not make their philosophical underpinnings an explicit element of training; the underpinning assumptions of what constitutes knowledge and how it is 'found' are more often implicit in the research methods. However, education is not a discipline – it is interdisciplinary (see Figure 1.1). This means that education as an area for enquiry is impacted on by different disciplinary perspectives which overlap.

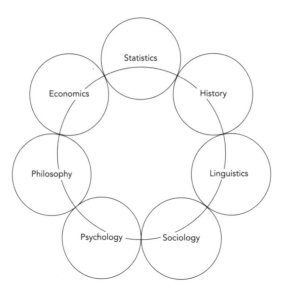

Figure 1.1. Education as an interdisciplinary field – many disciplines converge on educational interests.

This is perhaps what leads to debates about, and sometimes denunciations of, different methodological approaches within educational research. However, it is important when engaging with research in education that we attempt to understand and embrace these different views of knowledge and the methodologies which emerge. It is by developing an understanding of these different perspectives that we can begin to positively engage with and critique the work of others. In this sense, being 'positively critical' means to understand and engage with research from other philosophical traditions, even if our own beliefs are quite different. In the long run we may attach less importance to such work, or even discount particular perspectives, but by widening our horizons and developing multiple perspectives our thinking will be more informed and rigorous.

Becoming research literate

Research methods is an area of rich conceptual and knowledge content. This means that to develop a deep, critical understanding takes time and involves a great deal of sustained effort. To read and engage with research at a critical level requires a level of research literacy – that is, the ability to understand the positioning of research, the assumptions underpinning it and how this has influenced the resultant change. We argue that to develop a good level of research literacy requires three elements (summarised in Figure 1.2):

1. *Knowledge.* A working knowledge of research methods, from philosophical traditions/foundations to the practicalities of research design, is crucial for understanding both others' research and also for developing our own research projects. Without any knowledge we are at serious risk of producing poorly designed and, hence, unreliable and invalid research. When reading research, a lack of knowledge also leads to an inability to assess the degree to which we are able to trust research outputs.

2. *Threshold concepts.* The theory of threshold concepts has become increasingly popular in higher education research since Meyer and Land popularised the idea in the early 2000s (see Meyer and Land, 2003). It rests on the notion that disciplines have particular conceptual frameworks and that some of the concepts involved are central and transformatory to our understanding. However, these concepts are often hard to understand well and may take much time and effort to engage with deeply. Research methods is no exception. Some of the concepts which are central to gaining a critical understanding of research methods include ontology, sampling and methodology, to name just a few. We therefore need to spend time developing our understanding of these ideas if we are

to engage critically with the work of others and develop our own research projects.

3. *Application.* Developing and carrying out research projects is not a pursuit for everyone. We don't believe that primary research activity is necessary for all educators, even if individuals are keen to develop their research literacy. However, the development of small-scale research can have advantages for developing a wider research literacy. Firstly, undertaking small-scale research is an experiential learning process in its own right, requiring us to understand how some of the concepts and knowledge we might have read about actually come together to form a process of investigation. To read about research allows for a good level of theoretical understanding, but to try it out gives us a deeper perception. It also leads to another important aspect of application – that of gaining insight into the complexities of decision-making, development and the messiness of research as a 'live' activity. By applying some of our emerging understanding, we can build a more critical and nuanced perspective when reading the work of others.

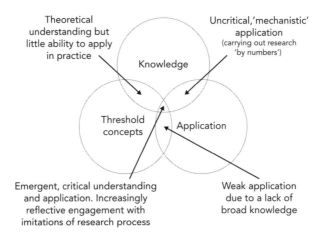

Figure 1.2. A simple model of research literacy.

So how do these aspects of research literacy come together? Figure 1.2 shows intersections between the various aspects. If we read about research methods and/or read research reports with no consideration of the practicalities or underlying conceptual frameworks used, then the level at which understanding takes place can be seriously compromised. However, even if there is an understanding of both knowledge and basic underlying concepts, there remains an inability to consider them in relation to the practicalities of actually carrying out research. If such practicalities are not understood and engaged with, the reading of research remains an essentially theoretical pursuit.

At the same time, conceptual frameworks offer a deeper coherence to knowledge. If this consideration of underlying and critical principles is absent, any attempt to use a knowledge base as a starting point for application has the potential to lead to 'mechanistic' engagement with research application. It is the deeper, conceptual understanding – together with a wide and well-developed knowledge base – which can, with experience, lead to well-considered and rigorous research projects.

However, we do need to accept that meaningful engagement with research across these three spheres takes time and experience. Research is a complex and highly contested area of human activity; becoming a good researcher, or even becoming research informed (i.e. having an ability to read and critically engage with research), takes time. Therefore, we would argue that it is perfectly possible to attain a level of research literacy by reading and reflecting on research, but to gain a deep, critical appreciation requires us to actually undertake research, however small scale. Whether the extra insights and engagement are worth the added time and effort is a question only answerable by the individual, in part, in relation to what they hope to gain from their interest in research.

Introduction to the remaining chapters

This book is offered as a discussion of some of the basic ideas in educational research, meant for those with little or no research experience. We sketch out some of the main features and concepts in educational research, whilst also offering advice on constructing single, small-scale research projects. As such, we hope that it allows readers to engage with some of the basic conceptual elements of research as well as offering a foundation of knowledge and application. This is important to us for two reasons. Firstly, we intend that those who wish to develop research-informed practice (i.e. to engage with research through the work of others) will gain some useful insights into the research process. Secondly, for those who actually wish to develop their own research, we hope it offers some basic frameworks and approaches to help create and execute simple, small-scale research projects.

The remaining chapters outline and discuss some of the main features related to understanding research and undertaking simple projects.

- Chapter 2 considers the role of ethics in educational research. We have started the main body of this book with ethical issues due to the importance we believe this has not only in designing research but also in acting as a basis for all engagement with research.

- Chapter 3 considers the central aspects of criticality in research, both in terms of reading research and also beginning to write well-considered and carefully constructed reports about research.

- Research is often the result of particular interests and questions individuals or teams of researchers develop from their own reflections and interests. Chapter 4 outlines the importance of context and interest as drivers for creating small-scale research and for engaging with the research of others. Having considered the contextual, we then go on to discuss how this might translate to research questions, which are the foundation for research project development.

- Chapter 5 explores some of the philosophical foundations of research before going on to outline some of the main methodological traditions within educational research. These are the frameworks which are often identified and outlined in research papers, and therefore some understanding of their characteristics and relative strengths and weaknesses will help both understanding when reading research papers and also in the development of basic frameworks when designing small-scale projects.

- Chapter 6 outlines some of the main techniques which are used to capture data. As such, it acts as a basic guide to data capture in small-scale research as well as providing a basis for understanding research literature.

- Chapter 7 tackles the difficult subject of data analysis. This chapter does not provide detailed instructions for carrying out analytical processes which can be used in educational research, but it does provide an overview to help with orientation.

- Chapter 8 offers some ideas concerning how to approach the development of simple small-scale research projects.

Chapter 2
Ethical issues in educational research

Introduction

The decision to foreground ethical issues as an early chapter in this book was a positive, conscious choice. Too often ethical considerations are given scant regard and seen as a mere practical detail, a stage to be 'got through'. We would argue that ethical considerations are woven throughout all stages of the research process, from the selection of a focus to the reporting of findings, as well as in the formulation of evidence-based recommendations for policy and practice. Good research is responsibly, rigorously and ethically executed.

Research in education, almost without exception, involves human participants, typically children, teachers, non-teaching staff, parents, school leaders or governors. As an ethical educational researcher, you have a responsibility to ensure that steps are taken at each stage of the research process to make sure that your participants are treated with care, their rights are respected and their welfare is paramount. You are also duty-bound to ensure responsible reporting of the research. This includes transparency in explaining how the data were collected, organised and analysed, and due caution in making claims based on limited or unrepresentative data.

If you have undertaken (or are undertaking) studies in educational research through a higher education institution, you will no doubt have come across the sort of pro formas researchers have to complete to gain institutional 'ethical approval' before embarking on a research project. These forms are often generic, tick-box style pro formas designed to cover everything from Shakespearean textual analysis to heart research, and consequently include questions that bemuse students in education or sociology by asking them to confirm whether or not, for example, they will be wielding scalpels or taking tissue samples from their participants!

It is quite common for novice researchers, eager to get on to the interesting part of their work – data collection – to see the ethical approval application process as just a hurdle to clear before the real work starts. However, ethical considerations should be at the forefront of the responsible, reflexive researcher's conscience in every facet of her work. Ethical issues need to be constantly under review, and so constantly on the agenda of research meetings, generating and maintaining an ethical mindset that informs decisions and discussions throughout the research process.

We discuss below some of the basic principles of conducting ethical research in education, and consider the need to manage your research to ensure ethical integrity in your work. Different ethical issues arise, some quite unexpectedly, in different research contexts, so it is not our intention here to provide a catch-all recipe to follow that will guarantee ethically sound research. Rather, we aim to raise some issues for consideration and to provide some pointers for reflection.

Basic principles of ethical research

Ethics is defined as 'the whole field of moral science'. Behaving ethically therefore means acting 'in accordance with the principles of ethics; morally right; honourable; virtuous; decent' (Oxford English Dictionary, 2007). In a research context, this entails honesty and a commitment to protecting people involved in the research from harm. In operationalising your research project in education, therefore, there are three fundamental principles to consider: consent, honesty and care. We discuss these below.

Consent

The principle of informed consent is key to ethical research in the social sciences. The underpinning idea is that participants have a right to know about the purpose of the research, how they are to be involved and how the data generated will be used, cited and stored.

It is common practice in educational research to write and send out a 'research protocol' letter to the participants who will be involved in the project. The letter should state clearly the aims and purpose of the research, what level of involvement is required, the time scale and the steps you will take to protect participants' anonymity and confidentiality. In assuring confidentiality, you should also be honest in admitting the limits to this – for example, there is always the possibility that people reading your report will recognise participants in your study from your description of them or from the extracts you include from their responses. It is advisable to explain to participants that you will take steps to protect their anonymity, such as using pseudonyms and changing the name of their school in the report, but you cannot give a cast-iron guarantee that they will not be recognised. With this in mind, participants should be given the chance to withdraw, in part or whole, the data they do not wish you to use.

The research protocol letter needs to detail how any data gathered will be stored and at what point it will be destroyed. As the researcher, of course, you then have a duty to act on your word. It is often the case that a consent form for participants to sign is attached to the research protocol. In cases where participants willingly give their consent, their agreement to continue cannot be assumed. It should be made clear in the consent letter that they have the right to withdraw from the research at any point and they need to be reminded of this, and given opportunities to do so, throughout the research process. For example, if you were conducting repeat interviews over time, it would be reasonable to ask before each phase of interviews for their agreement and to remind them of how the data will be used. Securing informed consent needs to be seen as a process rather than a hurdle. An example of a research protocol letter and a consent form can be found in Appendix 2.

This is all relatively straightforward when your participants are adults who are able to read and assimilate the purpose of the research and make an informed decision on that basis. When your research includes children, clearly other steps need to be taken. Gaining the informed consent of parents or carers as well as the school is important. Often, if the project focuses on classroom-based teaching and learning activities, it is sufficient to send a letter home explaining the purpose of the project and asking parents or carers to get in touch only if they do not wish their child to take part. In our view, though, it is also incumbent on the researcher to find a way to explain to the participants themselves what the project is about, how and why they might be involved, and to gain their agreement too. This means that the researcher needs to find a way to ensure the participants understand what is going to happen, and what they are actually agreeing to, so that informed consent is possible.

As educational professionals, teacher researchers are well placed to make decisions about how to do this ethically and we would not seek to advocate any one approach. For example, if you are involving your class in your action research project, you are probably best placed to know how best to explain what you are doing and gain your pupils' agreement. A common strategy is to explain the research project and assume consent, whilst giving participants the opportunity to opt out. This is not necessarily unproblematic in ethical terms. Teachers are in a power relationship with pupils and it could be difficult for a child to refuse to take part, especially if his parents have given their consent. Much depends on the relationship of trust between teacher and students. If a small number of children do opt out, this does not mean your research project cannot go ahead; it simply means that you cannot draw on data relating to the children who have not consented.

In all cases, the researcher needs to ensure that no pressure is brought to bear on potential participants to take part in the research. This might not be pressure directly from you as the researcher. For example, you might approach a head teacher and ask for her help in recruiting teachers in her school to participate in your research. Whilst this seems like a reasonable way to gain access to a school, in practice staff being asked by their head teacher to participate in a project might feel compelled to agree. It is important to find a way to invite, not expect, people to take part, and to tolerate non-responses as inevitable. It is sometimes difficult to accept that not everyone will share the enthusiasm of the researcher for the project. From your angle, it might seem that there is absolutely no risk involved for the participants in your study. From the perspective of potential participants, however, it might look very different and there may be very good reasons why they do not wish to take part. As Thomas (2009: 149) comments:

> [Children] may ... not want to lose respect amongst their peers; [professionals] may ... not want to be seen to be taking part in a project that

has the endorsement of the management, or, conversely, not want to be seen to be critical of management.

Invitation, not insistence, would seem to be the message if you are to involve participants who have willingly given their consent to take part in your work, and this is, of course, particularly important if your intention is to focus on sensitive issues.

Honesty

Honesty in reporting findings and methods

A commitment to honesty and the care of participants and others affected by your research also needs to inform how the findings of your educational study are reported. It is common practice to employ pseudonyms when quoting extracts from participants' interviews in order to protect their identity. It is usually advisable to use a pseudonym for the name of the school or institution too and limit the geographical detail you provide about its location. Even so, it is not possible to promise participants that their identity is 100% protected. In any case, if interviewing children, safeguarding legislation takes precedence – it is not possible to promise children confidentiality. Just as teachers are obliged to report to the safeguarding officer any indications of abuse, suicidal thoughts or involvement in terrorism, so the researcher is bound by the same rules.

Neither can you fully guarantee that adult participants' identities will be fully concealed. It is quite possible that people reading your report might recognise their colleagues or pupils in the description of them or in the things they say. This is particularly likely in the case of high profile or unique individuals. For example, if one of your participants is the only black head teacher in a particular area, it would not be difficult for readers to work out who they were. This becomes even more of a concern if the data you are reporting might potentially harm participants' reputations. For example, perhaps the head teacher in question confides in you that he has had a number of nervous breakdowns or that he drinks heavily to alleviate the pressures of his job and his failing marriage. To report this risks damaging his future career, his credibility with his staff and his reputation in the area. It might even lead to his dismissal.

It may be too that the way you report your findings could potentially harm relationships between other individuals or groups of people. For example, you might undertake an investigation into the process of curriculum development within a particular case study school. It emerges from the study that the senior leader in charge of curriculum is viewed with suspicion by subject leaders and that his claims of consultative ways of working do not resonate with their accounts of how decisions are made in the school. If insensitively reported, this could open a Pandora's box for the school, irretrievably damaging working relationships.

Similarly, you have a responsibility as a researcher to ensure that the way in which you report your findings does not reinforce unhelpful social stereotypes. Well-meaning but ill-conceived and inappropriately reported research can damage particular groups in society – for example, by presenting black boys as predisposed to crime and violence or women leaders as having 'soft' skills rather than the heroic qualities and 'toughness' attributed to their male peers. Of course, the potential for harm of this sort should be considered at the research design stage, but at times surprising findings emerge and difficult decisions need to be made about what to report, what to leave out and why. For reasons such as this, an ethical mindset needs to remain constant in your work.

The reflexive researcher needs to pre-empt the potential for harm and make research design decisions that place participants' well-being at the core. Such considerations need to inform decisions made at every stage – for example, in framing the research problem, deciding on the research tools, writing the interview schedule and deciding what findings to report and how. It is your responsibility as the researcher to ensure complete transparency in reporting what you did at each stage in the research process, including how you organised and analysed data and how you selected what to include. Readers and users of your research need to be clear that you have not been selective in including only data that you wanted to use to make a point. This would constitute dishonest misrepresentation of participants' data. Manipulating the data to tell a story that suits your preconceived ideas is highly unethical and constitutes very poor quality research. There is less opportunity for this to happen in research accounts where the researcher has been transparent in communicating the details of the steps followed in the process. These considerations point to the intricacy of effective research and the need to spend time drawing up a research design to ensure ethical integrity in your work. You therefore need to allow yourself the time to problematise the research design in a slow, iterative process of reflection and action.

No deception

The researcher's commitment to honesty also implies an undertaking to ensure participants are not deceived in any way. An often cited and controversial study undertaken by psychologist Stanley Milgram in 1963 prompted much debate about whether or not deceiving participants can ever be justified. Milgram was interested in extending his understanding of obedience to authority. He invited members of the public to take part in a study, telling them the focus was on improving memory and learning. When the participants arrived, a man in a white coat (actually an actor posing as a scientist) guided them through the process. He explained that they were to fulfil the role of 'teacher'. In an adjacent room was a 'student' (also an actor) to whom the teacher should ask a range of questions. If the student answered the questions incorrectly, the teacher was required to operate a range of levers to administer electric shocks of increasing intensity to the student. No electric shocks were actually administered but the teacher participant did not know that. As they carried out the instructions given to them by the 'scientist', the participants heard increasingly disturbing screams from the student as the shock intensity was increased. Some participants expressed concern, upon which the scientist told them they should carry on. In most cases, they did, even though this was against their better judgement.

Milgram debriefed the participants after the experiment. However, much discussion amongst other researchers and academics focused on the harm done to his participants, who subsequently had to come to terms with the idea that they were capable of administering severe electric shocks to students on the say-so of a man in a white coat. Obedience to what they perceived to be authority caused participants to abdicate responsibility for their own behaviour. This experiment took place at a time when the world was trying to come to terms with events that took place during the Second World War. It had emerged that terrible acts were committed by concentration camp guards who claimed that they were merely following orders. In the wake of these events it might be argued that the insights gained into human behaviour through Milgram's work were sufficiently significant to justify the deception of his participants. The question is whether the means by which he generated these insights was ethically justifiable.

We are not particularly recommending that you take time out to read Milgram's work. However, the ethical issues it raises are crucial. Whilst researchers are free to define for themselves the areas they consider worthy of investigation, this needs to be balanced against researcher responsibilities to the people implicated in the research. It may even be that a commitment to honesty and a refusal to deceive research participants means that some types of research are not possible, or at least need to be refocused so that they are researchable in other, more ethical ways.

Care

Of course, the Milgram experiment is an extreme case, but the issue of ensuring that no harm comes to participants as a result of their involvement in our research is nonetheless important in education. Well-intentioned research can have unintended harmful implications for participants if insufficient thought is given at the planning and research design stage to participant protection and welfare. A few examples follow.

Eliciting narratives

Let's imagine a study in which head teachers are being interviewed about their lives and careers and how they came to be head teachers. One approach might be to use life history interviews – that is, to elicit narratives in which participants reflect on their past, present and anticipated future lives to tell the story of their career. This can be a very useful technique, generating rich, interesting life histories. However, for some people, revisiting past memories, for example, can prove painful or embarrassing. Prior to the interview, you would need to find a way to forewarn participants that life history narration can sometimes be upsetting for interviewees and that they should feel free to stop the conversation or withdraw from the study at any point. On the other hand, you would not want to over-dramatise and create the expectation in participants' minds that the conversation is going to be upsetting or that you are expecting them to share painful memories. This indicates the importance of reflecting on the implications of your research design for participants at the planning stage. This process cannot be rushed if the integrity of your research is not to be compromised.

This is a potentially tricky and sensitive area when working with adults; with children it may be fraught with ethical difficulties. For example, asking children to talk about their home background, upbringing and earlier life may trigger a range of upsetting memories or bring to the fore embarrassing problems that your participants would not otherwise choose to share with you. If you are undertaking research with pupils you know well, you are probably well placed to make decisions about what would and would not be suitable topics for discussion. If you do not know the children, it is probably best to be cautious or at the very least take advice from pastoral staff or teachers who do know the children well.

Control groups

An issue that comes up from time to time in classroom-based practitioner research is the use of control groups. We have had discussions over a number of years with teachers undertaking postgraduate research degrees based on their own classroom practice. In order to ascertain the effectiveness of a particular intervention, several teacher researchers have suggested using control groups. This means the teacher researcher identifies two groups of pupils, a test group and a control group. The intervention is trialled with the test group – perhaps a new teaching strategy or a set of activities in which pupils engage – and the control group carries on with their 'normal' classroom activities, the idea being to compare the two groups at the end of the 'experiment' to ascertain whether the test group has made more progress.

This approach is rooted in the scientific method, whereby a hypothesis is formulated, an experiment is designed to test the hypothesis and then the evidence is used to prove or disprove the hypothesis. In this kind of research single variables are identified and causal relationships are established. This is the approach used in randomised controlled trials (RCTs) which have become increasingly popular in educational contexts. However, there is a debate here as to the ethical consequences of using such approaches. They might be regarded as fine if you are a market gardener who wants to know whether the new fertiliser on the market will improve your tomato yield: you might use your usual soil for half of the plants, the fertiliser on the other half and compare the yield. However, learning is a highly complex area to study and involves human beings. It is highly improbable that we can isolate variables and establish causal relationships in a teaching and learning context with any ease. Moreover, in working with children, to deny one group access to experiences that may enhance their learning can be deemed as unfair and unethical, and probably contravenes equal opportunities legislation. Therefore, we would advise against using control groups in small-scale research and suggest instead that the interventions you try out with your classes involve all pupils. Ascertaining the effectiveness or impact of the intervention will involve drawing on a range of data, and this is likely to provide a deeper understanding of the learning process than comparison between two groups.

Use of visual materials

Many educational projects use a number of traditional social science research tools such as observation, interviews, questionnaires and documentary analysis. Increasingly, a range of visual methods is coming into vogue, as they offer interesting ways to harness rich data. One of the strengths of using visual methods is that participants have some control over what they might want to talk about and share in an interview. For example, you might want to gather pupils' perspectives on the learning and social environment in your newly built school. An interesting approach might be to use photographs as the basis for interviewing pupils. Instead of asking predetermined interview questions, you might ask your pupils to take photos and compile an album of pictures of places around the school that have some meaning for them in terms of learning and social life. This album might then provide the basis for a narrative in which pupils talk through the photographs they have included and describe their significance. This technique might afford fascinating insights into individual students' perspectives and experiences that you probably could not achieve through interviewer-defined questions.

However, care would need to be taken to ensure, for example, that the album did not include photographs of other children whose permissions, and those of their parents or carers, had not been sought. This sort of issue could be pre-empted by thinking ahead and carefully wording the instructions to participants that the photos should contain pictures of places but not people. There are other potential issues with this approach in terms of compromising anonymity if the photographs are to be included in the report. Again, these are considerations that would need to be thought through at the point of drawing up the research design, so that unethical data were not generated accidentally. Again, this brings home the point that ethical reflection needs to be at the core of the whole research process.

Self-protection

In considering participants' rights to protection from harm it is sometimes easy to forget that, as the researcher, you also need to ensure that you are not harmed or placed in a difficult position in the research process. All of the same advice applies to school-based research as to teaching. For example, if you would not normally see one child alone in your room at school for teaching and pastoral purposes, neither should you if you are undertaking research.

If you are going off-site, perhaps to conduct interviews, again the common sense advice might be not going alone to meet someone you have never met before in a remote place. In any case, it is always wise to let a colleague or your research supervisor know when you are conducting fieldwork and where, and to give them a mobile phone number so they can make contact. In most cases it will be a simple matter to make sure that you are not putting yourself in a dangerous situation. In some cases you may be able to draw on professional support services to negotiate access or chaperone you on visits for interviews or discussions for your research. For example, a postgraduate research student wanted to focus her research on a traveller community. This was not straightforward but with the help and advice of the local Traveller Education Service she was able to negotiate access, agree times and dates when she could visit, and was accompanied by a chaperone from the Traveller Education Service. She was also told by the ethics committee at her university that she should telephone her supervisor before and after every visit to confirm that she was safe and well.

If the subject matter of the interview conversations is, or could be, distressing for you as the interviewer, thought needs to be given to your own need for counselling and support. There are occasions when interviews elicit harrowing narratives. There are similarities here with some of the experiences you might encounter in school – for example, it can be very disturbing if a child discloses to you that they are being abused. Having reported this, it would be wise to think of your own support needs. The same applies if research interviews are upsetting. The potential for this should be considered at the research design stage and it should inform the sort of questions you ask and/or the way you frame your narratives.

We have tried in this section to raise some of the issues and provide examples of the sorts of issues that the educational researcher might have to think through to ensure an ethically sound research study. There is no prescriptive list detailing how to cover all ethical bases. Reflexivity on the part of the researcher is key to ensuring the ethical integrity of the work. A significant part of this involves identifying and managing one's own biases in the research process, as we now discuss below.

Managing researcher bias

A number of scholars (e.g. Thomas, 2009; Sikes, 2010) highlight the importance of stating researcher 'positionality' in your work. This means acknowledging your personal starting points – for example, why are you interested in this research? Why is it important to you? What values, beliefs and political convictions underlie your interest in this area? What biases do you bring to the research?

Honest acknowledgement of your own biases is the first important step in ensuring your work is ethically devised and conducted, but mere acknowledgement of bias is not enough on its own (for further discussion on research bias see Chapter 4). There is a need to manage your personal biases and involvement in the work to the benefit, and not the detriment, of your study. This has implications for every stage of the research process.

Managing researcher bias in the research design

Many researchers, if not all, embark on research projects focusing on a topic they are passionate about and that matters personally to them in some way. This is important in sustaining interest and the motivation to continue and finish the project. The downside is that researchers may come to the table with what is essentially a campaign rather than a research project. Some seek to 'prove' what they already believe, to show the world the 'evidence' that what they know to be true is true. This is not a research project. A research project needs to be designed and framed in a sufficiently neutral way such that unexpected findings, including findings you don't like, can emerge.

A good starting point for drawing up your research design is to come up with two or three research questions. What exactly are you trying to find out in this study? These questions need to be phrased so they are free from unquestioned assumptions, biases and researcher expectations. There is a big difference between, for example:

Why are girls so uninterested in maths?

And:

What do Year 9 pupils perceive to be the interesting and engaging aspects of learning maths?

What do Year 9 pupils perceive to be the discouraging or demotivating aspects of learning maths?

Is there evidence of gendered trends in pupils' responses to maths?

Another important difference here is that the question, 'Why are girls so uninterested in maths?' is not researchable, whereas the second set of three research questions do lend themselves to research – that is, it is possible to identify what evidence would be needed to answer the questions and devise tools to gather it. The research design for such a study might involve using pupil questionnaires or interviews, or both. Of course, in order to answer the final research question a large number of pupils would need to be involved, which might not be feasible in the context of one school or one class. However, emergent evidence from, say, the interviews with children might provide some interesting pointers about what pupils find engaging or off-putting in maths lessons, and it might even be that there are some apparent gender differences. You would, of course, need to be very cautious in making claims about gender differences based on a small sample.

So, having framed the research questions so they are neutral, assumption-free and researchable, you now need to think about how you will manage your personal biases in the data collection process.

Managing researcher bias in data collection

By being aware of your own biases you can be alert to ensuring that the sorts of questions you ask in an interview or include in a questionnaire are not leading and do not have inbuilt biases. For example, to ask a child, 'What is it you hate about maths?' clearly rests on a certain assumption, whereas, 'Tell me about a really good maths lesson you've had', could glean much more useful insights.

Another important issue in any research, but particularly for teacher researchers working with children, is that of researcher power. Of course you want to establish a relationship of mutual trust and respect with the participants in your study, but it is also important to acknowledge that you hold a great deal of power in the researcher–participant relationship. Even if you are involving adults and peers in your work, as the researcher you define and frame the study, you select the questions you will ask, you make decisions about how to organise the data, you prioritise what you see as important and you decide how and what you will report as your findings. This puts you in a position of authority. As a teacher involving children in your research, the power and influence you have over the process are considerably heightened.

So, it is highly important to manage your own behaviour as a teacher researcher when working with children. Not only do you need to design interview schedules or questionnaire questions that are not leading, but you also need to ensure that your behaviour as a researcher is not leading either. For example, in conducting an interview you might inadvertently convey through body language (e.g. by smiling or nodding) that you 'like' what a child is telling you, thereby encouraging them to continue by giving particular types of answers or saying what they think you want to hear in order to please you. By adopting a more neutral stance you allow the interviewee to talk about what is important to them, with the result that the data you gather is more authentic. Self-awareness and researcher reflexivity about your influence on the research process are key parts of conducting your research ethically.

Managing researcher bias in organising and analysing data

It isn't only in devising the study and collecting data that researcher bias can influence the findings. It is highly important that your processes for organising and analysing your data are rigorous and transparent, so that the findings you eventually present are valid and trustworthy.

If we take the example of interview data, it is generally viewed as good practice to make sure that interviews are recorded and transcribed in full so that the participants' voices and perspectives are properly heard. If undertaking thematic analysis some form of coding is likely to be used. Ethically, our advice would be to ensure that everything in the transcript is coded, unless there really are completely irrelevant passages. (For example, in one of our studies, a recording includes an interviewee talking to her cat from time to time! Much as Tiddles appreciated the attention, it added little to our understanding of the participant's career decisions, so a decision was taken not to code these sections.) By coding everything you are less likely to cherry-pick – that is, to select quotes you like and are interested in but which are not particularly representative of the data overall.

In connection with this, it is important to remember that not only can the researcher have an impact on the study, but participants can affect the view of the researcher. For example, you might find that one of your participants very much impresses you with their lucidity and wisdom and that their interview is much more interesting than any other. The temptation is to over-represent them in the work. Whilst their data may be interesting, if it is idiosyncratic it needs to be acknowledged as such and not presented as though it is typical of the sample.

There are simple devices you can use, even with highly complex data, to chart similarities across a sample. For example, you might create a simple matrix, identify themes and for each theme show in which participants' transcripts it appears, as in the table below.

Participants

Theme	John	Bill	Sally	Kath	Jean	Gurpinder	Lee	Total
Maths is important if you want a job	2	1	1	1	1	2	1	9
Group work is fun	0	1	2	1	2	2	1	9
I enjoy maths homework	2	2	1	0	0	2	1	8
Working independently is enjoyable	2	2	2	1	1	2	0	10

Key: 0 = no evidence of this, 1 = some evidence of this, 2 = strong evidence of this.
Table 2.1. Themes matrix for summarising data patterns.

This is a very simple tool. It is helpful in providing you with an overview, but it is less helpful in giving you a picture of how important each theme was for each participant, or how long they talked about each theme and in how much detail. However, it can help to guard against over- or under-representation of individual participants in your analysis and report.

Finally, it is your responsibility as a researcher to be absolutely transparent about every stage of the research process when you produce your written report. Explain what you did, in what order and why. Be honest about the limitations of the work as well as the effect of your own biases, and how you sought to limit this. If you have presented a sufficiently detailed, transparent account of your work, it should be possible for another researcher to replicate the study in a different context.

Managing researcher bias in reporting findings

If your research design is effective it should be capable of generating findings that you had not expected or anticipated (rather than simply confirming your pre-existing beliefs). This includes the possibility that findings emerge that you do not particularly like. However, the fair reporting of findings that are grounded in the data is a big part of ethical research.

A corollary of this is that in undertaking research with human participants, the ethical researcher needs to adopt a non-judgemental stance. It is not the role of the researcher to criticise her participants' beliefs, actions or perceptions. For example, in a study of how government policy has impacted on the work of teachers, it might surprise you to find that a participant in your study lauds the decisions of the coalition government and sees former Education Minister Michael Gove as a visionary who transformed education for the better. You might have a different view but it is not your role as the researcher to attack your participants. Ultimately, ask yourself whether you would be happy if what you have written about your participants had been written about you or a member of your family. This should indicate whether or not you have accorded due respect to your participants.

Some potential ethical quandaries to consider

What do you consider to be the ethical issues arising from the proposed research projects outlined below? What would be your advice to the researcher proposing each study?

Project 1: Case study

A school-based project is planned in which the focus is on the self-perceptions, self-esteem and self-identities of disaffected pupils. The intention is to compare the children's perceptions with those of their teachers. The case study will include unstructured classroom observation, interviews with pupils and a focus group with teachers.

Project 2: Participant observation/ethnography

A project is proposed focusing on the pedagogies and practices in a large language school in the south of England. In order to obtain an authentic 'insider' understanding, the researcher proposes to register as a student in the school and undertake covert observation of classes, recording sessions on a digital voice recorder. He will also interview students about their experiences of the school.

Project 3: Photo-stimulated narratives

The project seeks insights into young people's experiences of private education in an English boarding school, their developing identities and their view of their future selves. Participants will be asked to bring in photographs which are important to them in terms of their experience of boarding school, how they see themselves now and their hopes for the future. They will be asked to discuss the photos in an interview and explain their significance.

Project 4: Case study

Aware of an increasing problem of bullying in her school, especially amongst Year 8 girls, a teacher researcher plans to investigate online bullying. Her methods include interviewing children she thinks might be being bullied as well as those who are doing the bullying, looking at the children's Facebook pages and asking them to share text messages with her in which bullying messages have been sent or received.

Summary

In this chapter we have identified some of the key principles in conducting ethical research – those of consent, honesty and care. We have provided some pointers for reflection by giving examples of the sorts of ethical conundrums that can be implicit in undertaking research in educational contexts. We have sought to emphasise that ethical issues are interwoven into the fabric of the research process and need to be addressed at every stage. We have argued that there is a need to be transparent in explaining the steps taken in devising the study, collecting, organising and analysing data. We have stressed that researcher self-awareness and reflexivity are key to ethical research and managing personal biases in the process of research and in the reporting of findings.

Chapter 3
Critical reading and writing

Introduction

In this chapter we discuss what we mean by criticality in the context of educational research. We consider the links between reading, writing and the development of thinking, and argue that writing needs to be a part of the research process throughout. We suggest that critical friendship can be a powerful resource in your development as a writer and researcher. We provide some suggestions for critical engagement with the literature in your area and for drawing up your theoretical framework, which will also inform your methodological decisions. We discuss briefly how you might present and critically discuss your findings in the light of the theory you have selected as relevant to your work. Finally, we provide some pointers to ensure your writing is clear and coherent, as well as appropriately critical.

What do we mean by 'criticality'?

Criticality in the context of educational research might be defined as the ability to question, to evaluate, to assimilate complex ideas and to form new perspectives. It implies an element of scepticism in its most positive form – that is, the ability to unpick implicit assumptions and identify the weaknesses as well as the strengths of an argument. It means recognising when the claims made by a researcher are justified and when they are made without due foundation. So, becoming more critical means developing your ability to appreciate the value and validity of others' work, as well as to identify its limitations and shortcomings.

Criticality also means developing your ability to synthesise ideas from a wide range of sources and to combine them in novel and insightful ways to offer fresh perspectives on an area. Research in the field of education offers considerable potential to draw on sources from a wide range of subjects and disciplines. For example, you might take theoretical perspectives from psychology and sociology and combine them to create an original theoretical lens through which to view your topic of study. Alternatively, you might view your data through two or three different theoretical lenses to create a multi-layered analysis. Whilst this scope for bringing together diverse perspectives and ideas might be daunting, it offers the freedom to think creatively and to fuse ideas in ways that are innovative, contemporary and tailored to the specific purposes of your unique study.

Criticality also implies the ability to be reflexive in your own work and to evaluate rigorously your own research practices and writing. As an educational professional you are well placed to offer nuanced understandings that integrate your practical experience with theory and research within a clear analytical framework. This requires an ability and a willingness to step mentally outside of your daily work to view what can be taken-for-granted assumptions through a critical lens and to reflect critically on your practice and experience in the light of your readings and emergent thinking. The development of criticality can lead to a powerful change in practice, informed by your critique of policy and new understandings of teaching, learning and the leadership of schools.

Critical thinking, writing and friendship

From an early stage, taking the time to write is a very important part of undertaking research. As you engage with research, reading and thinking about your area of study, you will develop your thinking and understanding by writing regularly about the ideas you are developing, the concepts emerging from the literature, the methodological considerations implicit in your research and the potential implications of your work for policy and practice. It is never too early to start writing. Kamler and Thomson (2006: 2) discuss the notion of 'research as writing', emphasising that the process of writing is integral to thinking, meaning-making and developing research understanding. It is not, they emphasise, something that happens *after* the research.

Much of the writing you do during the research process will be messy and developmental. This is perfectly normal – no one can sit down and write a perfect report in one sitting. There will be much redrafting. This is not a sign of failure, but a stage in a highly complex process. Like slow-cooked food or fine wine, quality research takes time to mature and develop, and there are no quick-fixes. We don't know of any writers, even very experienced writers and researchers, who can rattle off a paper in one go. It takes time, patience and the ability to take risks, get things wrong and start again. Redrafting becomes a way of life. It can actually become an enjoyable and satisfying part of your life!

Writing and research need not be solitary activities. We would strongly recommend building critical friendships with other researchers in your area. Critical friendship is a lot more than tea and sympathy or cheerful support. We would suggest getting into early habits of providing each other with constructive critical feedback on each other's drafts. To begin with, you could use the criteria below as the basis for giving one another helpful critical feedback. A few bullet points against each criterion should be adequate to give feedback:

- Clarity of language and expression.
- Critical engagement with, and evaluation of, literature/theory/ concepts.
- Development of argument.
- Two or three strengths.
- Two or three points for improvement.

By articulating how your colleague might improve, and what they are doing effectively already, you will become more aware yourself of the areas you are developing well and those you need to work on.

Lots of people find it hard, especially at first, to give or receive critical feedback. We are just too polite: we don't want to hurt others and we don't want to be hurt by critical feedback ourselves. It's important to see that the feedback is not an attack on the individual, but a constructive analysis of the strengths of our work and the areas that could be improved. Critical feedback is important in researcher development and an integral part of the research world. In order to progress everyone needs access to quality, constructive feedback.

If it is too time consuming to read others' work, or if in the early stages you are very uncomfortable with giving and receiving feedback, start by meeting up with your colleague once a week or so to discuss ideas and your developing thinking. Two people in regular dialogue can create ideas and forge perspectives neither could achieve alone.

Critical reading and writing in your research

A logical starting point for any research study is to ascertain what other writers and researchers have already established about your proposed topic of study. For this reason, most research reports normally include a literature review. The purpose of this is to set out, with reference to the work of other writers, what is already known about the area of investigation, so that you can identify with confidence the gap in knowledge your work will address and the original contribution it will make.

In drawing together your readings and bringing them together in a literature review, you need to demonstrate the skills of synthesis and analysis. For example, this might mean you would need to identify the main themes emerging from the literature and organise the discussion around these, identifying where there is consensus and where there are different or opposing schools of thought. For example, a literature review based on factors affecting women teachers' career decisions (Smith, 2007) was structured around the following headings and subheadings:

Societal factors affecting women teachers' career decisions:

- Gendered processes of socialisation.
- The motherhood ideal.

Institutional factors affecting women teachers' career decisions:

- The gendered educational institution.
- Direct discrimination.
- Endemic, covert discrimination.

Individual factors affecting women teachers' career decisions:

- Values and motivation.
- Personal aspirations and perceptions of school leadership.

- Personal agency and career decisions.

Synthesising the writings of a range of authors in this way requires a systematic approach to recording the key points made by individual writers, as well as points of comparison and differences between writers. It may be that an annotated bibliography will suffice, but it may also be helpful to create a simple matrix on which you note down which authors have written on each theme. For example:

Themes	Writers			
Gendered socialisation impacts on how girls and women see their future possibilities	Stanley and Wise (1993)	Millett (1969)	Sharpe (1976)	Pfister (1998), etc.
Motherhood is a major factor framing women's career decisions	Jackson (1994)	Mann (1995)	David and Woodward (1998)	Aveling (2002), etc.
Schools are gendered institutions	S. Acker (1994)	J. Acker (1992)	Newman (1994)	Morely (2000), etc.
Sex discrimination is still evident in the educational workplace	Shakeshaft (1989)	S. Acker (1994)	Wilson (2005)	Neill (2007), etc.

Table 3.1. Summary matrix of themes in the literature related to authors.

This provides a starting point for bringing together the thinking of a range of writers in a systematic way. However, the skill of writing critically implies more than listing who found what, who said what and who agreed with whom. The temptation when reading research papers in your area of interest is to look only for the findings and to ignore the methodological and theoretical discussion. The result of this is that less well-written literature reviews feature summaries of the foci and findings of each study without any analysis, synthesis or reflection, and with no links made between the works cited or even back to the writer's proposed topic of study. The result is a disjointed list of largely unrelated statements rather than a coherent account of the theory and research in the area to date.

Inevitably, the quality of the studies, reports, books and chapters you read as you develop your literature review will vary. Not everything that gets published is of a high standard. As you read, maintain a healthy scepticism: you do not have to accept everything you read as valid. This does not mean being negative or cynical, but having an evaluative framework in mind that helps you to make some judgements about the quality and validity of the work. For example, you might consider:

- The quality of the argument, including whether there are any gaps in the development of the theory.

- Whether the work is based on implicit, unquestioned assumptions.

- Whether the writer oversimplifies complex issues.

- The robustness of the research design, including how the data were gathered and analysed.

- Whether the claims and conclusions made are borne out by the evidence presented.

- The writer's worldview and the implications of this for the research design, analysis and conclusions. For example, might a different interpretation of the results have been possible? What might a researcher with a different perspective have argued?

- Where the work fits with other literature in the field or schools of thought on the topic.

- Whether anything is missing from the study.

As well as evaluating the quality and validity of the research you read, make a judgement about its relative importance to your work. Not everything you read will be useful or relevant, so you will need to decide what is valuable and should be included and what should be discarded. Making decisions of this sort is part of taking ownership of the argument you are developing. The important thing to keep in the forefront of your mind when compiling a coherent literature review is to be clear about what your line of argument is, to take control of it and to use references in the literature you have consulted to support your argument.

Theoretical framework

By engaging with the work of others it becomes possible not only to ascertain what is already known about the topic you want to investigate, but also to engage with some of the thinking that underpins different approaches to research and different understandings of knowledge and truth. Your reflections on your readings, and on your own work, will help you to identify the theoretical lens or lenses through which you will view the topic under scrutiny, and which, combined with your personal values, experiences and beliefs, form your worldview. It is unlikely that you will 'find' your theoretical framework before you have taken the time to complete a sound and thorough literature review.

The theoretical framework is the viewpoint from which you will look at the topic you are seeking to understand and at the findings that emerge from your study. It brings together a number of concepts drawn from your readings of theory and research. 'Theory' is hard to define, but at a simplistic level we might agree that it is an explanation of something. Selecting theories that have some potential to explain what is happening in your findings is of primary importance, and it may be that you will need to bring together a range of theories and a multi-layered analysis to offer a full explanation. The theory you select needs to be appropriate in the context of your work, as it will be key to the sense you make of your findings. So, whilst you might be fascinated by Marxist theory, if your study is focused on developing second language learners' use of question forms, Marxist theory is unlikely to offer much of relevance. If, however, your work focuses on the proletarianisation of the teaching force in neo-liberal Britain, you might be on to something. Even then, it is wise to consider alternative perspectives as well and relate the theories you have selected to these – that is, consider how the phenomenon you are looking at might be viewed differently.

So, the theoretical framework might also be seen as a lens through which you choose to view something. A former student expressed this very nicely by explaining that her theoretical framework was the 'pair of glasses' she put on to look at her topic. You might, for instance, adopt a perspective based on Marxist theory or feminist theory. In this case, you would need to explain the assumptions on which your work rests, as well as defining what Marxism or feminism means for you in the context of your work. For example, in the thesis cited earlier (Smith, 2007: 96–97), feminism was defined as follows:

> The work has an explicit feminist agenda, which, for the purposes of this study, I define as meaning that it is based on certain assumptions. The first assumption is that we live in a patriarchal society, that is, one in which male power and dominance are endemic. The second is that the institutions within which women teachers work reflect patriarchal society in microcosm. The third is that what passes as 'objective' knowledge is actually the subjective construction of a largely white, male, middle class body of academics. Within this body of 'knowledge', women's voices, perspectives and experiences have been largely excluded or ignored. There is therefore a need to redress the balance by introducing those perspectives.

The discussion that followed then considered what this meant in the context of the particular project:

> This means that the study has certain implicit aims as a piece of feminist research. It aims to focus on the experiences of women, with a view to improving conditions for women. It aims to give voice to women and represent their experiences to balance the white male bias in the construction of knowledge. It aims as well to involve participants in a research process that is emancipatory and empowering.

The theoretical framework implicitly informs methodology, and you will need to show in your writing the links between the two. Methodology is to do with the philosophical underpinnings of your work and links to your worldview and theoretical framework. In the case of the thesis cited above, a lengthy discussion ensued in which the case for using life history methodology was developed, on the basis that it gave voice to a relatively silent group of women and provided the freedom for the participants to reflect on their lives, defining for themselves what the important factors had been in framing their career decisions. This allowed more scope for the participants to take control of the conversation rather than responding to a researcher-led agenda. As such, the approach was consistent with the feminist aims of the project. So, the aims of the project, the assumptions on which it is based, the worldview of the researcher and decisions about methodology need to be explicit and the links between them made clear throughout the report.

If using 'grand theory', such as that of Marx, it is important not to apply this uncritically in your work. Its usefulness, or its ability to account satisfactorily for your findings, may well be limited. There is no need to be overly reverential of the 'big names'. Indeed, you would need to show you had reflected on the limitations of the theory as well as the strengths, and to show how and where your findings were consonant with Marxist theory, as well as where there was dissonance and why. You might even suggest some modifications that might need to be made to the theory in the light of your findings.

Discussion and analysis of findings

There are two main ways in which educational researchers present and discuss their findings in a research report. The first approach is to present a straightforward statement of the findings first, and then, in a separate section, provide the analysis and discussion of the findings – that is, the researcher's interpretation of the findings and the sense they make of them. In this case, the findings section would be descriptive and the discussion section critical. The second approach is to merge the findings and the discussion so the findings are both presented and interpreted in the same section. This requires critical writing.

In this context, writing critically means writing constructively, not destructively. It involves interpretation, sense and meaning-making, explanation and the linking of ideas. This is the point at which you are involved in building your own theory. Importantly, it means writing your findings as part of a narrative. It may be helpful to think of your research report as a story you are telling, with a start, middle and end. The discussion of findings is an important part of the story, for which you have been setting the scene throughout. Thomas (2009: 233) comments:

> it is here that you will set your analysis in the context of everything that has gone before, including your literature review. You will be tying strands together, intertwining ideas, weaving a fabric that is sometimes called 'theory'.

Of course, you will need to be clear about what your findings actually are before you can interpret and discuss them. This may mean that you need to decide what is very important, less important or not important, and perhaps order and present them accordingly. You might start with the least important and progress to the more important, or vice versa, and you might decide to leave out some of the findings or include them in an appendix.

We argued earlier that writing is a way of developing your thinking and is a part of the research process. Becker (1986) suggests that this is a way of making your thoughts visible, advising that the best way to start is by writing a first draft without using the delete key – writing as fast as you can write and think, without worrying about structure, typos, references and so on. Then redraft. Becker's argument is that with the ideas on the page you can see your thoughts, which you can then reorder, rephrase, correct, refine and make more coherent. There is no need to be so perfectionist that you try to get it right first time. You can rewrite it as often as you want to or need to.

Writing clearly and critically

Effective, communicative writing is clear, coherent and well structured. Language is economically used. Sentences are short and easy to understand. In the process of redrafting and refinement, there are a few ways in which you can make sure your writing becomes more clear and coherent as well as critical and reflexive. Some simple suggestions and things to be aware of are outlined below.

Avoid jargon and convoluted language

There is a tendency sometimes for inexperienced researchers to try to sound 'academic' by using lots of long words and overcomplicated sentences. It doesn't help, and it will alienate your readers. Use your own words where possible and explain your ideas in clear, simple, accessible language. There certainly should not be anything in your work that you don't actually understand yourself!

Try to avoid jargon. Where it is essential to use specialist vocabulary that is not in common parlance, define key terms clearly and be consistent in how you use them. Look at this example:

> Given that personal agency, which might be defined as women's capacity to take control of an aspect or aspects of their lives (and therefore careers), is central to feminist theories constructing women as other than victim of circumstance, the need to view these findings through the lens of resistance to oppressive structures as opposed to the more prevalent view predicated on the 'glass ceiling' notion of 'barriers' to women's progression, becomes apparent.

How did reading this make you feel? What is happening here is fairly typical. The writer is coming to terms with some highly complex ideas. Trying to express them results in a bafflingly convoluted sentence, with multiple sub-clauses and brackets. It is typical of an early draft. Some work would need to be done to break the long sentence down into shorter sentences and to define certain of the terms. Here is a reworked version:

> For the purposes of this paper, 'personal agency' is defined as the capacity to take control of an aspect, or aspects, of one's life. In the context of this study, it is used to refer specifically to women's capacity to take control of their own career decisions.

> Feminist theories relating to women's career decisions might be divided into two main groups: 'glass ceiling' theories and theories of 'agency and resistance'. 'Glass ceiling' theorists argue that women's career progression is impeded by certain barriers, for example, discrimination. Theories of 'agency and resistance', on the other hand, emphasise instead the ways in which women *actively resist* the factors limiting their freedom in their daily lives.

> Therefore, in order to understand the full range of factors impacting on the career decisions of the women in this study, it is important to consider not only evidence of the existence of barriers to women's

progression, but also indications of their resistance to those barriers. (adapted from Smith, 2007)

In the edited and revised version, key terms are defined and related back to the study. Two main schools of thought on the topic are introduced in summary form, giving hints as to the wider argument to be developed in the study.

Check your grammar

It is perhaps surprising that grammatical inaccuracy so often features in written accounts of quite sophisticated research. Of course, language evolves and the rules change in accordance with common usage. For example, apparently it is now acceptable to split the infinitive (the most famous example of earlier abuse being provided by *Star Trek's* trailblazing usage of 'to boldly go'). In general, though, it is unwise to boldly break grammatical rules, even if *Star Trek* got away with it. A few common errors and things to look out for in your own work include:

- Subject and verb mismatch, e.g.

  The philosophical basis of the project, and the researcher's own biases, *has* to be taken into account.

  The philosophical basis of the project, and the researcher's own biases, *have* to be taken into account.

- Grammatical imbalance in the sentence, e.g.

  The implications of this research for policy are far reaching and it is necessary to effect progress.

  The implications of this research for policy are far reaching. Consideration needs to be given to the steps that might be taken in order to effect progress.

Make sure each paragraph communicates a key point

Paragraph writing is a skill in itself. As a rule of thumb, try to ensure each paragraph communicates one main point. Often, as researchers are developing their thinking, there is a tendency to pack too many points into one paragraph without actually developing any of them. Look at this example:

> Bourdieu's notion of social capital is useful to this study. Young people develop aspirations throughout their lives, and parents, teachers, schools and friends can influence these as well as media and magazines. Teachers need to be aware of how what they do impacts on young people. Poverty and wealth also frame aspirations.

You can see that the germs of several ideas are planted in this paragraph. However, no apparent link is made between the different elements and the writer seems to assume his readers know why he is putting these ideas together. We don't because he hasn't provided an explanation. It is also impossible to see what the main point is here. Indeed, each point is worthy of at least a paragraph. Look at this developed example of one of the points:

> Bourdieu's notion of cultural capital offers scope to develop a different theory about how and why young people develop the aspirations they do. He argues that the dominant classes in society have more 'cultural capital'. This translates into different levels of educational attainment so that the children of the dominant classes enjoy greater success in school and have higher aspirations.

Now it is much more apparent where the argument is taking us and we start to see how this crucial theory will feature in the work. Refinements of this sort come through redrafting, the process by which we refine our thinking as well as our writing. A useful technique to check coherence of the argument, when you have a nearly-there draft, is to try to write one sentence per paragraph that sums up the key point of the paragraph. If you can read the sentences and discern a coherent story, this means your argument is coherent and well organised. If you can't – it's time for a redraft!

Match subheadings to content

Depending on the sort of writer you are, you might start with a plan, draw up a structure of headings and subheadings and then start writing under each section heading. Or, you might be a more organic writer who sits down to write, developing your thinking as you go along, so you don't actually know what you are going to write when you start. In this case you probably allow the structure to emerge from your writing. Whichever way you do it, it is likely that the sections and subsections will change as you develop the work. You need to remember to check that the subheadings you use actually match the content of the section or subsection. We often see structures of subheadings that look logical when we skim read over a student researcher's paper, only to find that what is actually included in the discussion doesn't do what it says on the can. Here's an example:

Gender issues

Much inequality in education relates to unspoken assumptions about what children enjoy. Teachers make decisions based on limited access to resources and often inadequate initial teacher education. Indeed, often nowadays there are a lot of untrained teachers who are also very overworked and do not have the time to plan differentiated activities.

The problem here is that the author probably thinks the paragraph does match the heading, because in her mind she has discussed issues around gender. However, she has done this in a way that only she understands, assuming readers will make the same connections and leaps of logic that she does. Be aware that you need to spell out for your readers why you are making the connections you are and link them to the subheading as well as to the rest of the argument.

Eliminate overstatement and redundant phrases

When you edit drafts of your work, seek to identify and eliminate overstatement and get rid of redundant phrases and sweeping statements. All of us are in the habit of using pointless words and useless phrases. Here are some common examples and possible edits:

- 'It is a fact that …'

  e.g. It is a fact that head teachers juggle numerous responsibilities.

  Better: Head teachers juggle numerous responsibilities.

- 'It is important to point out that …'

  e.g. It is important to point out that there are still fewer women than men in the most senior posts.

  Better: There are fewer women than men in the most senior posts.

- 'It is well known that …'

  e.g. It is well known that there is a shortage of aspirants to headship.

  Better: There is a shortage of aspirants to headship.

- 'Nowhere is this more true than …'

  e.g. Women are under-represented in leadership and nowhere is this more true than in UK secondary schools.

  Better: Women are under-represented in the leadership of UK secondary schools.

In eliminating overstatement, you could also make a conscious effort to moderate your emphases. This means avoiding the overuse of adjectives like 'significant', 'important', 'crucial', 'vital' and so on:

e.g. It is significant that women are under-represented in management, and important to consider the reasons why this might be. This crucial research is vital and timely.

Better: Women are under-represented in management. This research investigates some of the reasons for this.

Better still: This research investigates the under-representation of women in management.

Be your own editor

Edit your draft. Bear in mind the following checklist, adapted from Eggleston and Klein (1997: 15):

- Check grammar: make subjects and verbs agree.

- Check apostrophes.

- Check spelling (don't rely on your spell checker).

- Check clarity.

- Limit use of relative clauses that break up sentences.

- Use words for precision not length (e.g. 'try' is as good as 'endeavour').

- Avoid sloppy and verbose writing.

- Write a crisp abstract.

- Ensure you have followed presentation and referencing guidelines to the letter.

Summary

In this chapter we have discussed what we mean by criticality in the context of educational research. We have emphasised that thinking develops through writing and critical friendship, and recommend that both need to be woven into the research process from an early stage. We have provided some pointers for critical engagement with the literature and deciding on a theoretical framework for your study. We have suggested this will have implications for your methodology. Finally, we provided some practical guidance on developing clarity and coherence in your writing.

Chapter 4
Thinking about the basics

Introduction

The reasons which lead people to decide to be involved in research vary. Some research is developed as a result of personal interest or academic curiosity. Often, research is pursued to help answer specific questions which arise through the identification of problems or issues. The questions themselves come from many different sources. For example, some come from reading the literature which already exists in an area. By understanding pre-existing evidence, and the gaps which have not been considered, questions can be designed to explore and investigate these areas where we lack insight.

However, the majority of small-scale practitioner research comes from more immediate practice-led development concerns. Reflection can lead to important insights which can in turn lead to new practice. Whilst reflective development can be successful, it can also result in bias and the belief that practice has been improved when there is little actual evidence to support such assertions.

In this chapter we consider the basis for interests in research and the biases we need to consider and avoid in developing those interests. We then discuss the important matter of context, before going on to describe how to develop a framework for asking good research questions as a basis for research design.

Interests

Interest in carrying out research can originate from many different sources. As we have seen, much research is the result of individual curiosity. Because research takes a lot of time and effort, it is natural that individuals will only undertake the required activity if they have a good set of reasons and interests to do so. This interest may be the result of professional work or purely due to natural/academic curiosity. There may be an element of practice which is troubling or perhaps an area of work which they would like to focus on to gain deeper insights. Research may also stem from a want or need to investigate a question which occurs due to particular organisational issues, which in turn may be the result of data analyses.

Because small-scale research in practice-based settings such as schools can often develop through personal need or interest, we need to be careful to develop research which is well constructed and which attempts to overcome initial biases. As interest in research has developed in schools and the wider educational community, so there has been a growing focus on the problem of bias – almost to the point of paralysis, where any discussion or investigation of issues is accused of one or more biases from an increasingly long list!

Biases do need to be considered because the interest which drives research can lead to problems, but part of the work of good researchers is to be aware of the biases which might impact on their work and understand how to minimise their effects. We could argue that all research is biased in some way, be it choosing one focus or topic over another or the methodological and data collection tools used. The important issue is how we identify bias, attempt to limit it (we can't eradicate it) and report transparently to enable others to engage with and assess the validity and reliability of our work for themselves (see Chapter 7). However, given that we tend to research ideas that we are interested in, some of the more common biases to consider when developing (or indeed reading) research include:

- *Confirmation bias*: This type of bias occurs when an individual interprets information based on previous assumptions and experience but excludes other available data. This can be problematic in two ways. Firstly, when developing research we might focus on a particular intervention or evaluative focus due to our preconceived assumptions about an issue. It will often be perceptions and experiences which lead us to look at a particular area, but once we have done so we should try to carry out some form of reconnaissance to ensure that we are informed of the wider situation rather than replying purely our own viewpoint. Reconnaissance can take the form of informal discussions or more formal use of interviews, work scrutinies or questionnaires, but the intent is to open our eyes to a wider focus than our own internal narrative.

Secondly, when interpreting the data we have collected, we need to make sure that we analyse fully and systematically to ensure that we don't just cherry-pick the data that suits us. For example, if we are evaluating a new teaching approach we have developed, we cannot emphasise the 20% of positive reactions and hide the 80% of negatives just because we believe in the idea!

- *Selection bias*: If we are invested in our research then it can become all too easy to select participants/respondents who we believe will be receptive to it. This is particularly the case when interviewing students about curriculum change or pedagogic developments. There can be a tendency to choose those who are both articulate and/or who might be expected broadly to agree with the development of the new approach. We need to be open in reporting how participants have been sampled (see Chapter 6) and how this might skew our results. In reading a paper, if sampling is not openly discussed then it is difficult to assess the results presented.

- *Question bias*: The questions which are asked within a piece of research have a fundamental bearing on the process. This is true both in terms of project research questions (see later in this chapter) and also where constructing questionnaire/interview questions. Questions can easily make assumptions or be leading (i.e. can point the respondent to 'correct' answers) (see Chapter 6). Therefore, again, good research will make clear the research questions used and also the questions asked during data collection.

- *Design bias*: The way in which data collection frameworks are designed can also lead to bias – for example, by favouring one tool over another, a different dataset will be captured. One way of trying to counteract this is to use more than one data collection technique which then allows the researcher to triangulate (i.e. compare the results gained from one technique with those from another). This then begins to build evidence and confidence in the results.

- *Analysis bias*: Once data has been collected it needs to be analysed rigorously. In any analysis there will be biases, as it is a natural by-product of sifting and selecting the data for particular purposes (i.e. to answer the research questions that have been posed). Instead, the researcher needs to make clear what the purpose of the analysis is, how the data has been analysed and the techniques used to interrogate the data (see Chapter 7). Any research you read should make these processes clear if the evidence is to be given weight.

As well as making biases and research approaches clear to the reader, it is also important, particularly in smaller scale research, to clearly outline the context of the research.

Context

When reporting research we should give a clear outline of the context. In larger scale studies this might include the general location/region as well as the overall characteristics of the organisations included. In small-scale research we need to give a well-defined account of the setting in which the research has taken place, as this increases the validity of the findings by helping the reader to understand in quite some depth where the research has occurred. This means they will be able to make decisions when reading your work as to whether it is valid and also the degree to which it is applicable to their own context.

A clear statement of organisational contexts might include major characteristics, such as the size of the organisation in terms of staff and students (where applicable). The socioeconomic and ethnic make-up of the area and organisation may also be relevant in relation to some research agendas, as well as the geographical area. You don't need to cover every last characteristic, but include anything relevant that relates to your research project. In fact, the information given needs to be carefully selected so that the organisation cannot be easily identified, on ethical grounds, unless all participants and the organisation itself are happy for the identity of the organisation to be made public.

In addition to the organisational context, many smaller scale research projects might be focused on a group within the organisation, such as a year group or a class in a particular subject. Here, age, special educational needs and disability and/or English as an additional language may all be applicable contextual data, as might the posts held by teachers or the inclusion of teaching assistants within the setting. It is important that only relevant data is given, not just a list of all available characteristics.

The suggested areas for inclusion outlined above are given to help the reader understand the context within which the research took place. This adds validity to the research reporting and allows the reader to engage with the research process and interpretation at a deeper level. However, in writing contextual descriptions it is important to remember to check for information which might compromise anonymity and confidentiality.

Finally, research reports should include the context of the researcher themselves – what is called researcher positionality (see Chapter 2). Where the researcher is also a member of the organisation, such descriptions should include an outline of their position within the organisation and also their relation to the participants. This last point is particularly important as it expresses the explicit/implicit power relationships between the researcher and the researched. If the researcher is interviewing students that they teach, for example, there is an obvious power relationship. Alternatively, a junior member of the organisation who is also a researcher might be interviewing a senior member of staff. Once again, the power imbalance might lead the researcher not to ask certain potentially sensitive questions. Researcher positionality should express these relationships and describe how moves have or haven't been taken to minimise their potential impacts.

Research questions

Having decided on the area you wish to investigate, you will almost certainly need to engage in a process of honing and refinement to turn your idea into a manageable project. Almost every study starts out wide and needs to be narrowed down to a sharp, clear, workable focus. For example, perhaps you have an interest in 'languages in the primary classroom'. This is a good starting point, but the focus needs to be sharpened in order to frame the research questions that will guide your work. 'Effective strategies for engaging *ab initio* language learners in the primary classroom' moves you closer to a specific focus and allows you to start thinking about your research questions.

In thinking about research questions, ask yourself, 'What exactly am I trying to find out in this study?' Spend some time formulating a small number of clearly focused research questions to guide the work. For example:

- Which teaching strategies are effective in engaging Year 6 pupils in oral work?

- Which resources and strategies encourage independent reading in the target language?

- How can authentic listening texts be effectively exploited?

- When, how and in what form should writing be introduced in the Year 6 language classroom?

Alternatively, you might develop one overarching question and a small number of sub-questions. For example:

Main research question

What do teachers perceive to be the impact of new-build schools on teaching and learning?

Subsidiary questions

- Is there evidence that new-build schools have a positive effect on student self-esteem?

- To what extent do teachers consider that new-build schools have impacted positively on student behaviour?

- Is there evidence that newly designed schools have been successful in reducing bullying?

- What other features of the new environment do teachers consider conducive to effective teaching and learning?

- Are there ways in which other improvements could be effected?

These are not perfect questions. Those you draw up to start with rarely are, and it may be that as you go along you will need to tweak your focus. The research questions you form will grow from your professional experience, your knowledge of the context within which you are working and your engagement with the literature in the area of interest. Practical considerations will also play a part in defining and determining research questions, in that the questions you devise need to be researchable within the constraints within in which you are working. In other words, if you are a lone researcher, working as a full-time teacher and without a research budget, it is unlikely that you will be able to undertake a national or international, wide-ranging survey on your area of focus. You might, though, be able to carry out an intervention with your Year 7 class or interview a few of your colleagues in school. Small-scale work is no less valid than large-scale studies, and it can raise important questions for further investigation.

There are instances when researchers might state a number of issues or problems they wish to address rather than formulate questions they want to answer. This is particularly likely in small-scale action research projects. In most cases, though, it is usually helpful, if only for the purposes of gaining clarity of focus, to form some research questions, worded as questions not statements. It is best to phrase these using language that allows for a range of answers to be obtained, rather than, for example, closed or yes/no questions. Some useful starting points for phrasing such questions might be:

- To what extent …

- What factors …

- How …

- Who …

- What …

Here are a few examples:

- To what extent is student disengagement from school a function of a narrowly examination-oriented focus in teaching and learning?

- What factors affect students' motivation to learn mathematics?

- How can schools better support disadvantaged young people?

- Who are the key adults influencing young people's perceptions and aspirations?

- What are the reasons for students' non-attendance at X Secondary School?

There are a few considerations to bear in mind as you draw up your research questions and start linking them to your proposed research design. The questions must be researchable. This means that they are worded in such a way that it will actually be possible to gather data that provide some answers to the questions. The questions need to be open and neutrally worded, not leading or biased, so that unexpected findings can be generated. Take, for example, the question, 'What damage have coalition government policies on education done to generations of children?' This may be a question you are aching to answer. However, it is not a neutral question: it is highly biased and, ultimately, not researchable. A more researchable question might be, 'What do teachers perceive to have been the impact of government policy on their daily work in schools over the last five years?' It is important that research questions are designed so that a range of findings is possible – that is, you are not setting out to prove what you already believe.

Let's consider a few early stage research questions from educational researchers.

Example 1

What factors affect the career aspirations of Year 11 boys who have been predicted grades D–F at GCSE?

This is a suitably wide, neutrally worded question that lends itself to research that might harness the perceptions of pupils, their teachers and their parents. The sample population is implicit in the question, and the rationale for this group is hinted at and would be expanded on elsewhere in the study. The question lends itself to investigation using a range of tools, which might include, questionnaires, semi-structured interviews and focus groups.

Example 2

What social and economic conditions lead to success?

This is far too unfocused and unwieldy to be researchable. 'Social and economic conditions' covers too broad an area to be addressed by a study in education and 'success' is not defined. This is not researchable in its current form and would need to be significantly honed down and focused much more sharply in order for it to become a project.

Example 3

Why are girls not interested in mathematics?

This is a very biased question in which a major assumption is implicit and unquestioned. It assumes that all girls are anti-maths and is neither researchable nor helpful. If the project could become positively worded and neutrally framed, it could become a study about engagement in mathematics, but in its current form it is hopelessly inadequate.

Example 4

Are there gendered trends in career orientations of management graduates from the University of Leicester in 2014–2015?

As with example 1, this is a very focused question in which the specific sample population is clearly identified. In working towards this question, the researcher is likely to have consulted the literature in the field to consider whether there are links between gender and career orientation. There are clear implications for research design implicit in the question. Tools likely to be used might include questionnaires and interviews as well as analysis of available data relating to alumni.

Consider these example research questions. Which of these are suitable and researchable as they are? Which need to be changed and how? Try to rephrase the unsuitable questions. Are there some that would be better if split into a main question and a subsidiary question or two?
How does government policy suppress the learning of disadvantaged groups?
What factors affect international students' ability to complete master's level programmes at University Y?

How does the study of yoga impact on staff well-being at the University of X?
Why are male students better at statistics than female students?
To what extent is there evidence of demotivation amongst undergraduates following the first year examinations?
What are the particular challenges faced by students who are also parents?

If your questions are carefully formulated, focused, clear, neutral and researchable, it will be possible to identify the data you will need to gather in order to answer your questions. At this stage you can begin to think about research design (i.e. the overall plan for the project). It should then be possible to devise effective, manageable research tools to gather the data you need (i.e. to come up with a research design that is fit for purpose). With this in place, you can then start to devise your research tools with a view to piloting and refining them, and make decisions about, for example, the order in which you might use the tools (e.g. questionnaire followed by in-depth interviews, interviews followed by broader survey).

Summary

In this chapter, we have considered the reasons we might have for undertaking research, which is often based upon our professional interests and the associated need to reflect on how we can minimise biases in our work. Context is also important in developing and explaining research, ensuring that the reader can understand the background to the research and thereby aiding the interpretation of results. Finally, we have outlined some of the considerations involved in developing research questions, which are closely linked to the methodological foundations of research projects as outlined in Chapter 5.

Worldviews and methodologies

Introduction

All research is based on a set of assumptions and principles. When you read research papers which report primary research, the authors will have developed a conscious strategy to capture meaningful and relevant data and results. This process is underpinned by a coherent framework known as the methodology of the research. The methodology used might be a survey, action research, case study, experiment or one of a number of other approaches, all of which relate in some way to a particular 'theory of getting knowledge' (Opie, 2004: 16).

Each methodology is supported by a set of principles which make assumptions about how the world is and what types of knowledge are possible about that world. Therefore, before we consider some method-ological approaches to educational research, we need to take a detour to consider some of the underlying assumptions about 'what is' (reality, ontology), what we can know (epistemology) as a result and the different worldviews or paradigms to which these lead.

Grappling with the philosophy of research

The philosophical foundations of educational research are often per-ceived as overly esoteric and very difficult to engage with, particularly for novices. This is partly due to the abstract language and concepts used, but it can also be the result of the literature which often uses inconsistent terminology. The philosophy of methodology is a huge area of research in its own right and here we can only offer a very brief introduction. However, this area of research literacy is extremely important in under-standing the logic and focus of research from the different traditions which together form the interdisciplinary field of education. There are three central principles to philosophical research in education:

1. Ontology: the element of philosophy which deals with questions of reality or 'What exists?'

2. Epistemology: the study of knowledge, what it is and how it can be acquired.

3. Research worldviews: shared views of how the world can be understood and researched and which are underpinned by ontological and epistemological assumptions.

Ontology

Ontology is a large field of philosophical study, but the essential question which acts as the foundation for study in this area is the deceptively difficult question, 'What exists?' In other words, what is the form of reality? In education this question can be further restricted to, 'What is the nature of the *social* world?' (as opposed to the physical world). There is a large spectrum of answers to this question and a great deal of debate concerning *the* answer – if there is one! At first glance this might appear to be a somewhat academic, even esoteric, pursuit, one residing a long way from practical research in the classroom. However, it underpins the conceptual understanding of research and many of the assumptions made by researchers as they develop their research projects.

A simple way of understanding some of the contradictory arguments concerning ontology is to consider the difference between objectivist and subjectivist foundations. An objectivist ontology argues that reality, or what is (i.e. what exists within the social world), is external and independent to us as individuals and researchers. In other words, reality is objectively real. Subjectivist ontology instead sees social reality as being constructed by individuals and groups, and hence is the result of experience and thought which is shared through language. As a consequence, reality is multiple, shifting and subjective as opposed to being independent, immutable and objective.

The difference between a subjectivist and objectivist ontology might seem to be of little practical importance, but these assumptions about reality have important impacts on the way research is understood and conducted. For example, if a researcher is interested in studying the effect of a new behaviour management technique, ontological assumptions will influence the form of the research undertaken. From an objectivist perspective it might be expected that the efficacy of the technique will be observable in some way and that by measuring the standard of behaviour, through some set of measurable variables, the relative success of the intervention can be determined and explained. Consequently, methods may be used which can quantify levels of off-task behaviour through proxy evidence of engagement such as the degree to which students are engaged in question and answer sessions, as well as the observation of particular negative behaviour types such as whispering, swinging on chairs and so on. By measuring each of these variables before and after the intervention has been implemented, the degree to which it has been successful can begin to be evaluated.

From a subjectivist position, the relative successes or otherwise of the intervention might be considered to be the result of changing social relationships and cultural processes. As such, the group with whom the intervention has been trialled might be asked about motivations, experiences and perspectives, with any important aspects of the changed reality of the class being identified as the result of the particular dynamics of that particular group. Such insights might be acquired through interviews (e.g. changed perceptions of behaviour) which would also take into account potential reasons for the changes occurring. Here, however, the insights are seen as specific to the group rather than easily generalisable to other contexts where the interaction of processes and people might give very different results.

As the discussion above emphasises, the assumptions we make about the nature of reality can fundamentally influence how we understand the research process, the types of approach we use in capturing data and the claims we can make about our findings. It should also be stressed that this section has outlined only two contrasting ontological positions. There are many others which you can explore if this is an aspect of research which interests you (see the further reading in Appendix 1).

Epistemology

Epistemology is the branch of philosophy which focuses on the theory of knowledge. In a research context it is directed towards what it is possible for us to know and what constitutes knowledge in our research. This then impacts on the assumptions we make concerning the knowledge we can claim to uncover. From an objectivist ontological position, which sees the social world as external and independent, data (if collected in a valid way) can lead to identifiable truths which are testable and knowable. However, from a subjectivist position of contingency and multiple and shifting relations the claim to knowledge is weaker. Contextual shifts mean that what counts as knowledge or truth may vary at different times and in different places.

Worldviews

If we are keen to develop our research literacy, either as producers or consumers of research, we need to understand something of the ontological and epistemological view and how these coalesce around the researcher's worldview. Creswell (2009) offers four contrasting research worldviews (also referred to as paradigms) as a basic framework for understanding approaches to research.

- *Post-positivism*: Positivism, which can sometimes become a pejorative term within the social sciences, is based on the theory that we can attain an absolute truth about the world. Positivism as a worldview is now almost non-existent and has generally been superseded by the post-positivist worldview. Post-positivism accepts that the uncovering of absolute and unchanging truths in social contexts is not possible, whilst retaining a sharp focus on the coupling of causes and effects. As a consequence, the use of experimental approaches is common within this worldview. These experiments are deductive in nature; in other words, experiments are used to verify, or otherwise, theories concerning the objective reality which exists around us. Experimental approaches can vary from relatively small-scale experiments to large-scale projects such as randomised control trials. Where data does not support a theory, it can be altered to aid greater clarity in understanding the world. Whilst there is no immutable link, much post-positivist research tends to be quantitative in nature.

- *Social constructivism*: This worldview is more often called interpretivism and is based on the idea that humans, as social agents, create their own realities. This has led researchers to attempt to understand the complexity of human life as opposed to focusing on a small number of chosen variables. The emphasis of this form of research is to interpret social, cultural and historical processes in their emerging complexity. As such, it is often (but not always) qualitative and small scale, and rather than evaluating theory the research inductively creates it from the observations made (i.e. any theories that are created occur from patterns/insights from the data).

- *Participatory*: Participatory research originated in the work of theorists such as Marx, Adorno and Freire who focused their interests on marginalised groups and a belief in social justice. Participatory worldviews problematise social constructivism by arguing that merely gaining insights into the complexity of social life is not enough because it is passive, whilst what is required is action and transformation. Participatory research sees measurement and evaluation as inadequate and advocates the development of understanding and transformation through action – the most well-known medium for this within education being action research.

- *Pragmatic*: Based on the work of Dewey and others, pragmatic research is focused on understanding, applying and enacting what works. 'Truth' is seen as what works at a particular point in time and does not rely on a single epistemological position. As a result, researchers emphasise research issues/problems and use whatever methods they believe will give them useful insights. As a consequence, mixed methods (a combination of quantitative and qualitative research methods) are often linked to this worldview. However, this is not an uncritical position, and it requires a great deal of thought and planning to ensure coherence and rigour in both approach and analysis.

Worldviews and philosophical positions are the basis for making decisions regarding methodology. The researcher comes to the development of a research project with particular assumptions about the nature of reality, the degree to which we can 'know' anything, and from these certain worldviews will emerge. As suggested above, different worldviews will tend to lead to the use of different methodologies.

Methodologies

The methodology of a research project bridges the research questions and data collection techniques which will be used. It is the framework which helps to make sense of research questions in a practical sense. For example, if a research question has been developed to find out the degree to which a large group of people agree or disagree with the implementation of a new intervention, a survey methodology might be the most appropriate framework for conducting the research. However, if the research question focuses on improving and developing practice within a given context, an action research approach might be more suitable. There are a number of different methodological approaches – we introduce some of the more common ones below.

Action research

Action research is often discussed in the singular, but it is actually a family of approaches with a set of consistent core principles. This is due, in part, to the fact that action research has developed across a number of disciplines and contexts, each of which has altered its form to suit their own needs. The following definitions give an idea of some of the core characteristics of action research:

> [Action research is] a form of collective self-reflective enquiry undertaken by participants in social situations in order to improve the rationality and justice of their own situations, their understandings of these practices and the situations in which these practices are carried out. (Kemmis and McTaggart, 1990: 5)

[Action research] is problem-focussed, context specific, participative, involves a change intervention geared to improvement and a process based on a continuous interaction between research, action, reflection and evaluation. (Hart, 1996: 454)

[Action research has] three important elements: its participatory character, its democratic impulse and its simultaneous contribution to social science and social change. (Meyer, 2000: 178)

A number of features of action research are highlighted by these definitions. At the core of the methodology is the idea of a problem or issue focus. Action research does not merely attempt to understand and describe a context but to change it for the better. As a consequence, it is often small scale and specific and emphasises transformation. It is also a participatory process with professionals, often working with others, attempting to use their different experiences, perspectives and expertise to bring insight and positive change to a situation. Finally, action research is linked to the concept of praxis. Praxis can have a number of subtly different meanings, but in this context it emphasises the need for a symbiotic relationship between theory and practice. Therefore, in action research, theory can be used in the initial framing of a project but with the explicit purpose of playing a role in bringing about practical change. In turn, the practical insights gained can be the basis for emergent theory that is specific to a context – what Jack Whitehead (2008) calls 'living theory'. Action research is also unlike other methodologies in that it is often carried out by 'insiders' rather than external researchers. Where external researchers are involved, this is often in the role of a facilitator or critical friend.

Action research is sometimes the first approach to research encountered and undertaken by practising teachers. Its practical nature makes it a positive choice as it can be used to interrogate and develop practice. However, it is also mistakenly thought of as being a simple research approach. This might be, in part, the result of the model of action research which tends to be introduced to teachers most frequently, that of Kurt Lewin (Figure 5.1).

Whilst appearing deceptively simple, this model is actually very complex if used critically. If misinterpreted, however, it can give the impression of a very loose and straightforward process whereby a teacher, or group of teachers, simply plan an intervention and then reflect on and discuss what they think has happened. This approach can indeed be taken, but

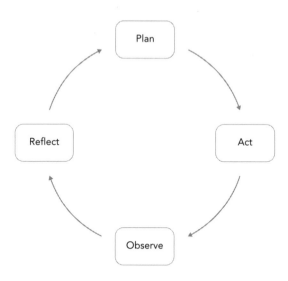

Figure 5.1. A basic action research cycle.

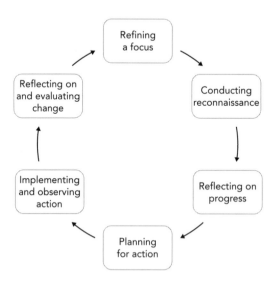

Figure 5.2. Modified action research cycle based on Townsend (2010, 2012).

with no consideration of the problem, other than personal reflection, biases can go unidentified and with no formal data collection the reflections may well have little evidential basis.

An alternative model of action research, developed by Townsend (2010), adopts a more substantial and critical approach, and is summarised in Figure 5.2.

One of the main differences here is the introduction of a reconnaissance step. Those involved in the research use this stage to gain information and data on the perceived problem. This helps to ensure that the issue they think exists can be properly characterised, thereby aiding the development of a meaningful intervention. As we highlighted in Chapter 4, we all tend to approach activities with a natural set of biases, so this reconnaissance stage is partly there to help us confront these biases.

The cycle then goes on to reconsider the intended focus in light of the new information which has been captured, before planning and implementing the intervention and then evaluating its success (or otherwise). This means that some form of evaluative data needs to be collected as part of the process. A data collection framework is developed and integrated into the planning of the intervention so that it has a meaningful structure and will gain insights into important aspects of the work which is to be carried out.

What this model demonstrates is that, if action research is done well, it is not a quick process that can be carried out unthinkingly; it requires a lot of thought, reflection and planning before, during and after the intervention. Well-conducted action research is not a simple task.

Example 1: S. I. Boon, Increasing the uptake of peer feedback in primary school writing: findings from an action research enquiry, *Education* 13(3) (2014): 1–14.

This research focused on increasing the uptake of feedback by children during peer assessment activities. The project was undertaken with a group of Year 6 students (10–11-year-olds) who had been observed to use very little peer assessment when developing their written work. The aim of the action research was to develop a more effective approach to peer assessment to ensure that the feedback given was used to improve subsequent written work.

Ideas for the intervention were based on insights taken from the research literature, including explicit training in giving feedback, time to act on feedback and opportunities for structural discussion between students.

The research was carried out with the whole class, which was taught by the researcher, and six children were identified for more in-depth data collection. The six were split into three pairs to characterise different writing ability levels. An activity based on writing a letter was then developed, taking into account evidence from the literature.

Evidence from the study included the work produced by the students, a response sheet used to show how students had reflected on feedback from their partner, observations of peer feedback as it occurred in the classroom, and informal interviews and mind mapping before and after the intervention to gauge changes in the students' perceptions on peer feedback. Data was thematically coded (see Chapter 7) and triangulated to distil major themes.

The data suggested that students' uptake of peer feedback increased due to:

- The use of time to ensure that students had opportunity to act on the feedback given whilst in class.

- The use of discussion to allow students to clarify what their partner meant when they gave feedback.

- The use of a reflective feedback sheet, leading to students thinking more about how they were using the information provided.

The results from the research were compared back to the literature. The researcher made it explicit that whilst the results were encouraging, the scale of the project did not allow for easy generalisations to other contexts.

This is a nice example of a small-scale project which was embedded in the practice and activities of one teacher and their class, and which, through the use of a number of data collection techniques, led to useful insights for developing practice. Whilst the researcher is explicit in emphasising the lack of generalisability to other contexts, the results are nonetheless of interest for others as potential places to look for new practice.

Action research has had various criticisms levelled at it as a methodology:

- As suggested above, good action research requires a lot of time over a long period. Many practitioners are extremely busy and therefore the systematic recording of data may be very difficult, resulting in poor quality evidence on which to base subsequent reflections.

- The insights gained from action research are not generalisable as they are context specific. Hence, they have limited utility outside of the immediate setting in which they have been developed.

- Some practitioners undertaking action research for the first time may not have a good understanding of research methods and therefore may use restricted or poorly designed data collection frameworks, which will negatively impact on the quality of the evidence collected.

Surveys

Surveys focus on perceptions and levels of agreement relating to an issue – that is, finding out what a population (see Chapter 6) thinks or believes about a given topic. Surveys are a relatively quick way to gain an insight into the chosen topic and tend to have a basis in quantitative approaches, although they can also have qualitative elements to them. They are likely to result in descriptive analyses of a topic but they can also be used to test hypotheses. Surveys make a great deal of use of questionnaires and structured interviews as ways of collecting data (see Chapter 6 for more on this).

An important aspect of creating a good survey is sampling. A truly random sample of the population is seen as the most desirable, but this can be very difficult to attain unless the whole population can be captured.

Therefore, careful consideration needs to be given to obtaining a fair cross-sectional sample of the population (see Chapter 6). One serious problem with surveys is response rates because small returns can impact on the validity of the research. However, it is unethical to compel individuals to reply to a survey request, which can potentially cause issues in the school environment where data may be used for more than one purpose. Participants need to be made explicitly aware of the way their data may be used, and they need to give their consent if they have actually filled in the questionnaire for a different purpose.

Analysis of surveys tends to make use of simple descriptive statistics such as the mean, median, standard deviation and interquartile range (see Chapter 7) and can be analysed and interpreted using subgroups and so on. More complex statistics, such as inferential statistics, can be used to identify and explain possible associations in the data.

Example 1: M. H. Lee and C. C. Tsai, Exploring teachers' perceived self-efficacy and technological pedagogical content knowledge with respect to educational use of the World Wide Web, *Instructional Science* 38(1) (2010): 1–21.

This study focuses on the development of educational technology and the use of the World Wide Web by teachers in Taiwan. The researchers use the theoretical framework of Technological Pedagogical Content Knowledge (TPACK), and in particular TPACK-Web (TPACK-W), as a basis for considering the link between subject knowledge, pedagogy and the use of technology in teaching. With this background to the study, the researchers investigated the degree of teachers' self-efficacy (i.e. self-perceptions, understanding of the web and their use of it for instructional purposes). To develop an understanding of teacher self-efficacy in relation to TPACK-W, the investigators used a survey methodology and developed a questionnaire.

The questionnaire was eventually completed by an opportunity sample (i.e. whoever was willing to complete it from the wider Taiwanese teacher population) of 558 teachers across all school phases from elementary to high school. The questionnaire included questions about teacher knowledge of the web, content of the web, pedagogic approaches using the web and attitudes towards web-based instruction. The sections mostly used Likert scale responses to statements which related to the identified foci. A further section captured basic demographic information to allow for comparisons of subgroups, such as gender, age and school type. There was also a set of open-ended questions which were used to explore teachers' opinions about web-based instruction. Before the final questionnaire was sent out for completion, the researchers sent a copy to an expert in the field for feedback, leading to changes being made to the tool before use.

On completion of the questionnaire, a series of correlation analyses were carried out across the data to gain an understanding of teachers' perceptions about the nature and instructional potential of the web. The results gained were interpreted as showing that there was a general lack of awareness of web-based pedagogies. Where more positive uses of web-based instruction were found, they were closely correlated to higher self-efficacy in teachers. Older and more experienced teachers were found to have lower overall self-efficacy relating to TPACK-W, and those with more experience of web-based instruction had higher levels of self-efficacy.

The example above shows how the use of a questionnaire to capture perceptions across a large sample of a population can lead to general insights concerning the work of teachers. The results function at a level of correlation but there is no causal power here; in other words, the research does not identify what is responsible for the patterns which have been uncovered. This would need to be the subject of further research. However, as a first step in understanding an issue, surveys can be a useful methodology to employ.

Surveys are not a perfect approach to research and a number of issues need to be taken into consideration:

- Any associations which become clear through statistical analysis only show correlation rather than causation. The associations do not show cause and effect associations but are sometimes incorrectly understood in this way.

- Response rates can be very low which leads to problems in data validity and potentially results in instances of over-claiming.

- It is important that the questions set are neutral and do not lead the respondents towards preferred answers (see Chapter 6).

- All too often, even when questionnaire returns are small, reporting will make use of percentages which can lead to careless or misleading reporting.

Case studies

The case study is relatively common in educational research, as it lends itself to looking in detail at one particular context. The emphasis in case study research is primarily on understanding how and why something happened, developed or came to be in a particular setting. The purpose of this might be to understand a critical issue or an unusual situation, to illustrate what is common or typical or to encourage aspiration by illustrating what is possible as an exemplar (Newby, 2010).

How you select your case depends on the purpose of the study. Cases are normally selected either because they are special or unusual in some way or because something has been working particularly well. Alternatively, it might be selected because problems or issues have been identified that are worthy of investigation. Nevertheless, the case study does need to be a self-contained phenomenon that is bounded in both space and time, and it should potentially offer wider relevance beyond the context itself – that is, the findings from the study might feasibly have applicability in other similar contexts. For example, you might want to undertake a case study of a school in which strategies are deployed to reverse the trend of underachievement in a particular group of pupils. This would be a useful investigation in itself, but it might also offer insights that could inform the work of other schools in similar socioeconomic circumstances. Whilst the primary picture that emerges will relate to the particular context and is not generalisable per se, it could possibly help us to understand other contexts where there are similarities. So, whilst in case study research the emphasis is on the particular, consideration will also be given to the potential applicability of the findings to other settings.

A case study should be sufficiently sophisticated to harness and make sense of the complexity that characterises a specific contextualised situation. It will tend to focus on explaining relationships and social processes in that context and situation and offer a holistic account of the phenomenon under scrutiny. The case could be a school, a class in a secondary school, a form group, a subject department, a teacher, a head teacher, a process, a programme, a policy and so on. In selecting the case to study, thought needs to be given to why it is worthy of investigation and why it is of particular interest, and you need to be very clear in explaining the rationale for the selection.

As with any sort of study, the chosen methods need to be fit for purpose – that is, capable of generating the data that will answer the research questions that drive the project. Because case studies harness complexity within real-life contexts, the most useful and rich studies will draw on many sources of evidence elicited through the deployment of a range of research tools. Yin (2009: 101) suggests there are six key sources of evidence on which case study research might usefully draw: documentation, archival records, interviews, direct observations, participant observation and physical artefacts. This list is not exhaustive. You might also undertake, for example, statistical analysis, parental questionnaires, lesson observations and policy document analysis. The point is that a case study that draws on multiple sources of evidence allows for a rounded view of the topic of investigation within the particular case study context, offering nuanced understandings of participants' lived experiences. This might entail a mixed methods research design or it might be more akin to ethnographic studies featuring, for instance, participant observation.

Where multiple tools are to be used, thought needs to be given at the research design stage to the order in which the various research instruments might be employed, in what combination and how the outcomes of one might inform the design and purpose of the others. For example, perhaps you wish to consider how a school has tackled the issue of sex education. It might be that you want to begin with a survey of parents' views and, having analysed the findings, then embark on a series of interviews with the head teacher, governors, senior staff, pastoral staff and so on to follow up on the issues raised. Having amassed the views of the concerned adults, you might then be interested in undertaking some observation of the classes in which sex education is being taught.

Example 1: Adapted from C. Mohamed, The shaping of socially responsible teachers. PhD thesis, University of Leicester (2014).

This enquiry focused on exploring mechanisms which challenge trainee teachers' assumptions of equality. Using a case study approach, Mohamed investigated whether experiences prior to the training process or the instructional pedagogies employed had the greatest influence in the shaping of socially responsible teachers.

The study was carried out on a primary PGCE programme with a total of 15 participants over two years. Semi-structured questionnaires and autobiographical accounts provided insights into participants' prior experiences. Participants' narrative reflections were evaluated in order to ascertain the degree to which their understanding of inequality and diversity impacted on their approaches to teaching and learning in the classroom. Further critical reflections identified which participants were capable of countering deficit stereotypes of pupils during teaching practice.

The study showed that it is possible to predict trainee teachers' propensity for social responsibility in the classroom. The analysis of data revealed that a trainee's sense of responsibility towards 'the other', coupled with the level of criticality employed in their reflective practice, is directly related to their capacity to become a socially responsible teacher. Coherent guidance and expectations employed through the instructional programme encourage socially aware trainees to act on this when teaching. The study confirmed the need to closely examine the coherence of initial teacher training programmes in guiding trainees' social justice awareness.

Carmen Mohamed was able to conduct research into her own practice as a teacher educator in seeking to develop socially just teachers. The methods used harnessed student teachers' prior experiences as well as their reflections on the pedagogical strategies that she and her colleagues used during the programme. A range of research tools – including questionnaires, autobiographical accounts and critical reflections – elicited a rich dataset. Her conclusions are likely to have relevance to other providers and implications for PGCE course design elsewhere.

Example 2: Adapted from G. Lalli, An ethnographic case study of the impact of food upon the learning environment at the Peartree Academy. PhD thesis, University of Leicester (2015).

This study investigated the impact of food on learning and social skills in an urban academy. The focus was on exploring the social and life skills which pupils develop through meeting, making choices, modelling teacher behaviours, eating and talking together in an inviting 'restaurant culture' rather than the traditional 'school canteen'. This ethnographic case study used a qualitative research framework for data collection. Research methods included interviews, observations and documentary evidence.

Four key themes emerged from the findings: 'meet and greet', 'modelling behaviour', 'social skills development' and 'the pedagogical meal at Peartree Academy'. Overall, the responses from interviews highlighted the differences of the restaurant from the traditional school dining hall. The observations allowed for distinctions to be made between the types of personas being presented in the school restaurant, which included 'the sociable teacher', 'the friendly midday supervisor' and the 'reserved teacher'. Overall, it was found that surveillance of the school restaurant was central to structuring potential learning opportunities for pupils. It was concluded that, like the traditional classroom, a school dining area also requires conscientious environmental adaptations in order for social skills to be developed.

This very interesting case study was conducted by Gurpinder Lalli in a school that was not his place of employment. He undertook an ethnographic case study, immersing himself in the life of the school in order to observe, understand and make sense of the relationship between food and the learning environment. Making use of interviews, observation and documentary analysis, he was able to ascertain that the positive strategies adopted by the school to promote a particular culture through food impacted positively on learning. This case study has clear implications for other urban academies in similar socioeconomic circumstances.

Potential weaknesses in case study methodologies include:

- The term 'case study' is not very well defined and can become a catch-all phrase for any small-scale research. This then loses the specific features of a case study methodology.

- Case studies are defined in some sense by their uniqueness and this can lead to criticisms that their generalisability is very poor.

- Case studies focus on depth as opposed to breadth, which can lead to a large volume of data if done well. Analysing and interpreting such a large body of data effectively can be very time consuming.

- Given the typical complexity of natural social settings, interpretation of case study data can lead to accounts which struggle to capture and report these complexities.

Experimental methodologies

Experimental approaches to educational research focus on gauging the effect of particular interventions. This approach has become increasingly popular in England in recent years through the work of the Educational Endowment Foundation which makes regular use of RCTs, a type of large-scale experiment.

Experiments are structured interventions which test a targeted change in practice. This methodology rests on the identification and testing of specified variables which are believed to have causal relationships with particular outcomes. A typical way of assigning causality in an experimental approach is to use two groups (the size of which varies depending on the scale of the experiment). One is exposed to a carefully designed intervention, whilst the other (the control group) continues to be exposed to a pre-existing activity. By using pre- and post-intervention testing, any statistically significant difference between the outcomes of the two groups can be identified and is deemed to show causal impacts of the variables relevant to the intervention. If it can be verified that the two groups have identical pertinent characteristics, then any difference in outcomes can be attributed to the intervention. Experimental methodologies tend to use complex statistical techniques to test the effects of the interventions, although it is possible to carry out useful experiments using only simple descriptive statistics.

The outcomes of experimental approaches are linked to the idea of uncovering 'what works'. Some would argue that experiments provide hard evidence for pedagogic approaches and so should be at the core of evidence-driven practices.

Example 1: K. Scheiter, C. Schubert, P. Gerjets and K. Stalbovs, Does a strategy training foster students' ability to learn from multimedia? *Journal of Experimental Education* 83(2) (2015): 266–289.

This paper investigates multimedia approaches to learning. Emphasising the importance of linking text and images to a consideration of cognitive theory of multimedia learning, the researchers claim that many instructional textbook processes do not optimise the advantage of using multimedia information. Whilst research does exist on optimising multimedia resources, there are far fewer studies considering how to help students make the best use of such resources.

The researchers set up a small-scale experimental design to test the degree to which students' learning could be enhanced by teaching them relevant learning strategies for use with multimedia materials. The experiment involved students learning about meiosis (a type of cell division) in one of two groups. At the start of the process, pre-existing knowledge about multimedia learning strategies, reading comprehension and domain knowledge (using mitosis, a different type of cell division, which had been previously taught to students) were measured. It was assumed that all students had no prior knowledge of meiosis.

A test group of 31 students were given multimedia strategy training designed to help them maximise their learning through use of multimedia materials. A control group of 33 students was given a training session which focused on issues other than the use of multimedia materials, including motivation and memory. After the training both groups were given multimedia training materials focusing on the process of meiosis which they were then asked to engage with before taking a test on the materials covered.

After the training, knowledge about multimedia learning strategies was retested and a set of 20 multiple choice questions on meiosis was completed using both text and image-based questions.

Both descriptive and regressional statistics were used to analyse and interpret patterns in the data. Comparison of the pre- and post-experiment results showed that the multimedia strategy training did improve student strategy knowledge but it had no significant impact on learning outcomes. This meant that whilst the students did gain greater knowledge about potentially useful strategies for using multimedia materials, they failed to apply these to the learning exercise.

The example above illustrates the basic process used in experimental methodologies and highlights that the results generally allow researchers to make claims concerning the degree to which identified causes or interventions can be shown to lead to desired outcomes. The outcomes are often reported in terms of affect sizes, or the degree to which the causal links analysed can be considered true or not. When positive results and causal relationships are identified, they may act as the basis for 'what works' forms of statement.

Whilst some researchers claim that experimental methodologies are important in their ability to show causal links, some possible problems have been identified in relation to their use in education:

- If the groups used in the experiment are small in size, then it is very difficult to ensure there are no differences between them, particularly as educational research takes place in complex, natural settings.

- Unlike medical RCTs, educational experiments are interpreted by the subjects as active participants rather than as passive recipients of an intervention.

- Control groups are not inert as they are still doing something rather than nothing, so the experiment may be measuring the difference between approaches rather than the quality of the intervention per se.

- There may be a lack of ecological validity. In traditional experiments, the laboratory setting allows for the control or eradication of variables which in classrooms cannot be easily controlled. It is extremely difficult, if not impossible, to create and maintain a consistent environment in a school environment.

- Do the results actually predict future impact, or only tell us what has worked?

- Is there a Hawthorne effect? Just being involved in the trial may actually have a positive effect in itself, regardless of the quality of the intervention itself.

Mixed methods

Mixed methods research has become an increasingly popular methodological approach in education over the past 20 years. The defining feature of this approach is that it makes use of both quantitative and qualitative data collection methods in a single research project. Historically, most research has used either one or the other, and some researchers argue that the two should not be mixed as they have different philosophical foundations. However, others argue that mixed methods research strengthens the process of triangulation (i.e. analysing and interpreting different sets of data relative to each other to look for patterns, inconsistencies and differences). Where these are found, the fact that more than one data collection technique has uncovered features is seen as giving the research greater validity. There is also an argument that quantitative and qualitative data can complement each other very well as they characterise different aspects of a single problem or issue.

There are a number of different ways in which methods in this form of research can be mixed. Two examples of relatively common approaches are given below to illustrate the type of mixing which occurs.

Sequential explanatory mixed methods

This mixed methods approach is often used when the context and nature of the issue is already fairly well understood. This might be through consideration of the research literature and/or previous research experience in the context under consideration. It starts by characterising the issues through wider quantitative data collection and then using qualitative approaches to add depth and explanation(s) of possible causal processes. In the quantitative element, questionnaires can be developed which cover pertinent issues and perspectives. The questionnaire is presented to a sample of the population and the results are then analysed to uncover numeric patterns. This generates data which provide a description of the issue, and may highlight particular points reflected in the responses.

An interview schedule is then developed to allow the researcher(s) to complete interviews with a subsample of those who completed the questionnaire. The interviews offer the opportunity for an extended consideration of the important issues highlighted in the questionnaire analysis, and enable deeper and more critical discussion with participants. This adds an explicit explanatory perspective to the research which the questionnaire alone would not be able to uncover. The quantitative data helps to reveal patterns which can then be exemplified and explained through the qualitative data.

Sequential exploratory mixed methods

In some research projects, the researcher(s) may not be able to identify which factors or issues might be important to pursue at the start of the project. In these cases, large-scale quantitative research may not capture data relating to important issues as they are not well known or understood. In these cases, the initial capture of qualitative data – for example, through the use of interviews with a sample of individuals – can be used to explore the nature of the issues. The interviews are then analysed to uncover the main factors which should be explored in questionnaires with the participants. Because the interviews help to pinpoint important factors, the questionnaire can be designed with this in mind, thereby making it a more focused and useful data collection tool. Once again, the quantitative data helps to identify patterns which can then be exemplified and explained through the qualitative data.

Example 1: E. Piggot-Irvine, Principal development: self-directed project efficacy, *Educational Management, Administration and Leadership* 39(3) (2011): 283–295.

This project was developed to evaluate a new independent study which was devised as part of a leadership development programme in New Zealand. The project aimed to introduce a context-specific enquiry process into the course to help leaders integrate and apply elements of their learning within their own work.

A mixed methods approach was used to evaluate the components of the programme, allowing triangulation of quantitative and qualitative evidence to investigate the relative success of the programme. A mixed quantitative/qualitative design was used to produce two online questionnaires. The first was administered at the mid and end points of the project and the second four months after its completion. Having collated the results from the first questionnaire, focus groups were used to extend and deepen the initial insights gained. In addition, individual insights from telephone interviews were used during the evaluation period at the end of the programme.

To gain further insights, observations were undertaken of presentations made following the project, and documentary analysis was completed on programme plans and outlines as well as session evaluations. The qualitative data was thematically coded

---

(see Chapter 7) and refined to tease out major themes within the data, and simple descriptive statistics were calculated to analyse patterns in the quantitative data.

Triangulation and analysis of the data indicated that there was an increase in understanding and appreciation of the leadership development project as it was developed, but there was also a lack of clarity concerning initial expectations which had been shared with participants at the start of the process. This suggests that when setting up independent projects of this type, it is important to give clear guidance on the 'rationale, expectations, quality criteria, scope and presentation requirements ... continuously throughout the project' (283).

The potential weaknesses of a mixed methods approach include:

- The time needed to complete the research in a mixed methods project can be greater than with other approaches and fieldwork needs to be carried out carefully. For example, if sequential approaches are being used, then analysis from the first element needs to be completed to allow for the planning of the second step.

- If different data collection techniques are used, the researcher needs to have a broader understanding of research methods to complete the research well.

- The researcher needs to understand how to carry out both qualitative and quantitative data analysis. This often leads to the need for researchers to work in teams to ensure that the required expertise is present.

- Some researchers maintain that the various methods cannot be mixed. This assumes that different methods are rooted in different philosophical paradigms that do not marry.

Summary

This chapter has considered the foundations of research projects. The worldview we develop concerning the nature of reality and knowledge are important in determining the forms of claims we make within our research. At a more practical, but associated, level we also need to decide on the most appropriate framework for our research. Research methodologies provide coherent and alternative frameworks for developing research projects and act as the basis for making decisions concerning the data we will collect, which is the focus of Chapter 6.

Chapter 6
Considering data capture

Introduction

Methodological frameworks provide the overall structure for a research project, embedding philosophical assumptions and outlining the approach. Within this framework, there are decisions to be made concerning the data capture tools which will be used and, as was alluded to in the previous chapter, the sampling strategy. In this chapter, therefore, we begin with an overview of several different approaches that researchers take when deciding who they will collect data from – in other words, creating a research sample. We then go on to outline some of the more common data collection tools.

Sampling

In most research projects one of the first big practical decisions is who will be involved in the research (i.e. the sample of people who will act as participants). This element of research is concerned with capturing data which is in some way representative of the wider context of the issue.

Research often makes use of a subgroup of individuals within the defined area of interest, rather than acquiring data from all those who might possibly be relevant. An example of this is the polling which occurs at general elections. The whole electorate in this instance is identified as the 'population'. The population is so large (measured in the millions) that it is not possible to ask everyone about their voting intentions. As a result, pollsters aim to create a representative sample of voters, usually numbering from 1,000 to 2,000 and chosen using various criteria, in an attempt to reflect the wider population. This process of selecting a small number of individuals from the overall population is known as sampling.

There are several reasons for using sampling. Besides a population being too large to capture all opinions/perspectives, sampling might be used to limit the volume of data collected. When research makes use of interviews, for example, the amount of time needed to conduct, transcribe and analyse the data is considerable. Therefore, if the population is large, sampling helps to limit the amount of data captured to a manageable quantity. This also highlights another reason for sampling – time. Not only can the volume of data become unmanageable, but the amount of time required to log, process and interpret data can become impractical. Related to the issue of time is the associated matter of cost, as this increases with both the sample size and the time needed to collect and analyse the data. Finally, sampling can be used to help capture data relatively quickly so that insights can be developed promptly – for example, acquiring data from an entire population may delay the publishing of the research. In some cases, a smaller, brief study can be helpful in gaining an initial understanding of a process or context. Where sampling is used, it is crucial that any report of the research makes explicit how this was achieved. A reader should always be able to make judgements about the validity of the data with which they are engaging.

There are various different types of sampling and, as with much in research, it is a major area in its own right. We outline some of the basic types of sampling below and show that there are a number of ways of deciding who could be involved in a research project.

Sampling can be classified into two broad types, both of which have a number of more specific approaches included within them.

- *Probability sampling*: Any form of sampling where the sample is in some way representative of the wider population – that is, there is a direct link between a group of individuals involved in the research and the whole population from which they are drawn. This form of sampling is perceived as being more rigorous as it can make a greater claim to generalisation and is often seen as being less biased in terms of the data captured.

- *Nonprobability sampling*: Any form of sampling where the sample is not chosen to represent the wider population. It may be selected to emphasise or highlight particular processes or it can be the result of the researcher having little choice in who is involved in the research. Nonprobability sampling can be criticised for being less representative and rigorous and therefore having less claim to generalisability. However, this form of sampling can be used to target specific individuals or groups who might be important within a particular context.

Probability sampling

There are a number of different types of probability sampling, all of which attempt to capture a representative sample in different ways.

Simple random sampling

When all members of the population can be identified (e.g. all students attending a particular school) a random sample can be created. This is often achieved through the use of a random number generator or through pulling names from a hat. Individuals are chosen until the desired sample size is reached.

Systematic sampling

Systematic sampling is a form of sampling which, rather than being fully random, selects every nth individual from a list. Therefore, if our list of students contains 1,200 individuals and we decided to sample 10% of them, we would select every tenth student in the list. However, to make it a true probability sample, the list itself needs to be randomised before sampling occurs.

Random stratified sampling

It might be that for our research we want to obtain evidence from all year groups within the school. In this case, we can split our list of students into separate year group lists. Each of these lists is then randomly sampled. The sample number in each year group can also be proportionate to the whole group, so if year group A is only 50% of the size of year group B then its sample is only half as large.

Nonprobability sampling

As with probability sampling, there are numerous different ways to use nonprobability sampling to obtain useful data within a particular context.

Convenience sampling

Convenience sampling relies on individuals who are willing and available to be involved in a research project. This type of sampling might be used in smaller qualitative projects where there is already little chance of generalisability. One of the main advantages of this form of sampling is that it allows relatively easy access to the sample group. However, self-selection of participants means the data collected can contain biases in terms of the perspectives captured, so this needs to be considered within the analysis and interpretation of the data.

Purposive sampling

With purposive sampling, the sample is selected in relation to relevant study characteristics. In a case study, for example, the researcher may wish to interview particular individuals due to their position in school (e.g. head teacher, year group leaders, learning support assistants). The sample will reflect the aims and research questions of the project but it may not represent the wider school population. This may be the method best suited to offering insights into the issues being researched.

Snowball sampling

In snowball sampling, the researcher identifies a small number of individuals who they believe represent the particular characteristics in which they are interested. These individuals take part in the research (e.g. completing interviews) but are then asked if they can link up the researcher with others who also meet the sample criteria, and the process begins again – hence the term snowballing. This form of sampling is often used where the target population may be unknown or where access to the population is difficult, perhaps due to the sensitivity of the subject or a lack of initial access by the researcher. As with convenience sampling, snowball sampling may lead to bias as the initial participants may steer the sampling in particular directions. However, it can be invaluable in allowing a researcher to make contact and conduct research with particular groups which would otherwise remain unreachable.

The examples of different sampling structures above offer a basic introduction to the different ways of identifying and engaging participants within research. However, like much of the research process, the choices made are a complex area for debate and contention, particularly in terms of their relationship to validity and reliability (see Chapter 7).

Data collection

As well as adopting a particular methodological approach and sampling strategy, the researcher needs to decide on the specific tools they intend to use to capture their data. There are many different data collection methods, so here we will consider only the more common mainstream approaches: questionnaires, interviews, observations and visual methods.

Questionnaires

The process

Whilst questionnaires are a widely used data collection tool, the development of a well-constructed and robust questionnaire is not a simple task. There are a number of issues which need to be considered in the design phase. At the point at which a questionnaire has been identified as an appropriate data collection tool, it is important that there is an initial overall plan which covers the issues discussed in the preceding chapters. The researcher should have already developed one or more well-structured research questions which will shape the main subject areas of the questionnaire. It is also essential to identify both the population and the sample to whom the questionnaire will be distributed. This is not only important in relation to deciding the size and nature of the sample but also in considering issues such as readability. For example, if a questionnaire is going to be completed by 11- and 12-year-old students, the use of high level language which some may not fully understand may lead to spurious results.

Having decided on the overall focus of the questionnaire through consideration of the research questions, it is then necessary to identify the ideas, concepts and issues that the questionnaire will cover in more detail. Pinpointing these foci is often the culmination of time spent understanding some of the pre-existing research in the field, as well as reflecting on the particularities of the context in which the research is taking place. Having determined the ideas, concepts and issues which the questionnaire should cover, it is then necessary to present these in the form of questions. The generation of questions requires both thought and time to ensure that they are both clear and neutral (see below).

The questionnaire should then be reviewed to ensure that the questions asked cover and relate back to the initial research questions. In the process of generating questions, the focus can sometimes drift away from the initial issue(s), so this form of review is important to safeguard the integrity of the research.

With the questionnaire complete, it is then preferable, where possible, to carry out a small-scale pilot. A pilot often involves asking a small sample, perhaps as few as five to ten individuals, to complete the questionnaire and then discuss it with the researcher. This process is invaluable in making sure that the questions have been interpreted by the respondent in the way that the researcher intended. In addition, those who take part in the pilot can also feed back concerns over poor phrasing or any other difficulties encountered. The researcher should use the feedback they receive to review and revise the questionnaire as appropriate. It is only once a questionnaire has been piloted and revised that it should then be used with the full sample that has been identified for the research project.

Structuring the questionnaire

Whilst developing a good questionnaire is not an easy process, with practice and experience it can be a very powerful tool for capturing the perspectives or opinions of a large sample of people (see the section on surveys in Chapter 5). When designing a questionnaire, it is helpful to think of it as having a single overarching focus which is then broken down into several different subsections, each of which concentrates on a specific aspect of the research. When designing the questionnaire, it is essential that the researcher already has a good idea of the type of analysis they wish to carry out once the data have been collected. Different forms of questions will allow different forms of data analysis, depending on the particular forms of quantitative data which are collected. In addition, the use of questions which rely on written responses allow for analysis which is focused more on qualitative than quantitative data.

One way of considering question types is to think of them as allowing either closed or open responses. Open questions normally require a written response which may range from a single sentence to a more extended piece of writing. Open questions are often used to gain a deeper understanding of an issue as they give the respondent an opportunity to explain or reflect on an issue, as opposed to merely providing numeric data. Text data can be analysed in various ways, including the use of simple quantitative methods such as identifying specific words or phrases which relate back to the question.

In contrast, closed questions make use of a number of different question types, all of which attempt to capture respondents' beliefs and perceptions in ways that allow some form of quantitative analysis. It is important that the researcher understands the form of analysis that a particular question type will enable them to conduct. It is not unknown for researchers to carry out inappropriate analysis if they have not considered or understood the type of data they are collecting (for a simple introduction to different types of data see Chapter 7).

Some of the most common forms of question used in questionnaires are given in Table 6.1.

Question type	Example	Type of data
Dichotomous Any question which offers one of two choices.	Would you use mobile phones in the classroom for teacher-led activities? ☐ Yes ☐ No	Nominal
Multiple-choice Any question where a series of choices are available. It can be stipulated how many choices can be made if more than one.	How do you usually travel to school? ☐ Walk ☐ Car ☐ Bicycle ☐ Bus ☐ Other	Nominal
Rank ordering A question asking the respondent to show a preference from a given list of choices.	Based on your experience, please rank the following feedback formats from 1–4 according to their impact on student learning. (Place 1 next to the format that has the most impact, 2 next to the format that has the next most impact and so on.) Remember, no two formats can have the same ranking. ☐ Written comments ☐ Verbal ☐ Grade ☐ Comment and question to reply to	Ordinal

Question type	Example	Type of data
Rating scales The most common question type asking the respondent to record their feeling or belief on a scale. It is important that the scale is not deliberately skewed (e.g. really strongly agree, strongly agree, agree, slightly agree, neither agree nor disagree). Also, an even number of choices can be given to avoid a neutral statement.	I was surprised by how much students learned in the research lessons that I observed. ☐ Strongly agree ☐ Agree ☐ Neither agree nor disagree ☐ Disagree ☐ Strongly disagree	Ordinal
Ratio data This form of question asks for measureable data and can have a zero response.	How many hours do you spend each day marking books?	Ratio

Table 6.1. Some common question types with examples and the type of data they provide.

Having decided on the types of question you want to use, you then need to construct the questions. This is perhaps one of the most difficult parts of the process, as it is very easy to write questions which can be challenged in relation to validity and bias. Some of the most common problems researchers face are leading questions and double-barrelled questions.

Leading questions are questions which force a certain response, for example:

Did you find the training:

☐ Outstanding

☐ Excellent

☐ Very good

☐ Good

☐ Generally good

It is important that the choices provided cover a full spectrum of potential responses and, where possible, it is useful to provide an 'other' category where the respondent can add their own response if the categories do not cover a full range of possible answers.

Another form of leading is the use of persuasive wording, for example:

Most individuals state that too much time is spent in meetings in the typical school week. Do you agree that too much time is spent in meetings?

☐ Yes

☐ No

Double-barrelled questions are questions which contain more than one question within them, for example:

How happy are you with your pay rise and your longer working week?

☐ Very happy

☐ Happy

☐ Neither happy or unhappy

☐ Unhappy

☐ Very unhappy

Such questions can often be identified by the inclusion of the word 'and', and need to be uncoupled and asked separately.

It is also important when creating a questionnaire to ensure that the format does not dissuade participants from taking part. It is good practice at the start of the questionnaire to have a brief introduction restating the aims of the research and setting out the ethical background to the study. For example, it should be made clear that any responses given will be confidential and anonymous, unless already agreed otherwise. It should also reiterate that the participant can withdraw from the process at any point, meaning that any participant can decide before, during or after completing the questionnaire not to be involved in the research. So, if an individual, having completed the questionnaire, then asks for it to be destroyed, the researcher must abide by their wishes. In addition, probability sample questionnaires usually include an initial section asking some basic demographic questions, such as year group, age, sex, ethnicity and so on, before moving on to the main body of the questionnaire. Beyond the introductory section, the questionnaire should be presented in a way that is clear and concise, whilst also, of course, capturing the desired data. Generally speaking, questionnaires which are overly long tend to have lower completion rates as participants either abandon them or complete them but give little attention to the questions asked and responses given.

Having piloted and completed the final design of the questionnaire, the last major decision the researcher needs to take concerns the mode of delivery. Traditionally, questionnaires were completed face to face or by post. However, with the advent of the Internet there are now a number of different online survey tools which can be used to deliver questionnaires electronically. In some instances, the mode of delivery is an easy choice – for example, if the questionnaire is being carried out within a school then it may well be that it is conducted in person during tutor time or within a particular subject setting. One of the advantages of completing a questionnaire face to face is that completion rates are often much higher than when individuals are asked to complete them in their own time. However, paper-based questionnaires require time to transpose the data into a usable electronic format. Conversely, online questionnaires can have a lower completion rate, but also have the key advantage that the data collected can generally be downloaded and exported into some form of database for statistical analysis immediately. So, different modes of delivery have different advantages and disadvantages. Whichever form of delivery is used, however, transparent and fair reporting requires the researcher to make it clear what the response rate of the questionnaire was so that the reader can assess and make judgements about the degree to which the analysis and interpretation of data is legitimate.

Interviews

The process

The purpose of interviews is varied but in most cases they are an attempt to capture in depth the views, perspectives and insights of participants. As with other data collection techniques, the information should be gathered in as transparent and unbiased a way as possible.

When evaluating different interview approaches, it is useful to consider the ways in which questions are presented to the interviewee. These can include:

- *Structured interviews*: This form of interviewing mimics the data collection approach of questionnaires. A number of questions are asked which may require shorter or longer responses but which do not deviate from the pre-established list. The interviewer simply reads out the questions and accepts the responses given without further probing.

- *Semi-structured interviews*: The interviewer has a set of questions about the chosen topic which they would like to ask the interviewee. However, each question is treated as a starting point for a wider discussion of that particular point. Therefore, having asked a pre-established question, the interviewer attempts to use extra improvised questions to open up and expand the thinking and perceptions of the interviewee. As a consequence, whilst the interviewer may come to the interview with six or seven questions, for example, they may end up asking a further six or seven supplementary questions which arise during the course of the interview.

- *Unstructured interviews*: In unstructured interviews the interviewer talks to the interviewee with no more than a generally identified area that is of interest. All questions are developed through the dialogue between the interviewer and interviewee.

These different approaches to interviewing rely on the degree to which a predetermined structure is necessary to meet the research aims. A structured interview will allow for more direct comparison between the views of respondents. Both semi-structured and unstructured interviews can elicit deeper insights from interviewees concerning the complexities and richness of individual contexts and perceptions; however, it becomes more difficult to ensure that the interviewer does not bias the process, as discussed below.

Interviews can be characterised in ways other than the degree to which questions are pre-established or developed within the interview. For example, one form of interviewing, called stimulated recall interviewing, relies on the interviewer and interviewee conducting the interview in relation to particular artefacts or video footage. For example, if students have been carrying out an activity within a lesson and the researcher interviews them by simply asking what they learned and how they attempted to complete the activity, the result might be very general responses. However, if the interviewer and student sit with the notes the student wrote during the learning activity, then this can be used to stimulate their memory of what they did and how they did it. Such stimulation is still imperfect but it nevertheless allows for a deeper engagement with the process. Other stimuli might include the use of annotated photographs, video footage or any other artefact which is directly linked to the particular area of interest.

Another approach to interviewing is used in life history research. Where stimulated recall interviewing tends to make use of semi-structured processes because there is a direct focus and a relatively narrow area of interest, life history research is very open and attempts to give the interviewee both time and space to consider and reflect on major issues in their personal history. Here, it is not uncommon for an unstructured interviewing approach to be used which may involve several interviews over an extended period of time. The intention is to focus on a general area of interest without closing down the narrative which emerges across the interviews. Whilst taking a great deal of time, this approach can result in a very rich set of narratives which allow for deep analysis and insight.

Planning for interviewing

As with any data collection technique, high quality interviewing is the result of careful planning and reflection before any data collection begins.

It is important that the questions have been generated in relation to the research questions developed for the study, so there is coherence between the project aims, the research questions and the data captured in the interviews. In any reporting of interview-related research, it is essential that the questions are listed in full so that the reader understands the focus of the study.

In terms of planning questions, many of the same potential pitfalls exist for interviewing as they do for questionnaires. Therefore, the interviewer must ensure that they do not use leading questions or biased questions (which assume that the interviewee will have a particular point of view), and they should also avoid asking complex questions which require multiple answers. In addition, where semi-structured or unstructured interviewing is used, the interviewer should make sure that any supplementary or unstructured questions are not framed in such a way that they lead the interviewee in a particular direction. This is a difficult skill to master but is necessary to ensure that high quality data is obtained. In addition, the interviewer needs to consider their demeanour during the interview. Body language, smiling, leaning forward, shaking the head and hand gestures can all result in leading the interviewee to give particular responses, so the interviewer needs to be as neutral as possible during the interview.

Interviewing is an intense process, so it is extremely important to spend time setting up the interview as well as conducting it. Firstly, it is good ethical practice to ask the interviewee at the start of the interview if they are still willing to be a part of the research rather than just assuming that prior informed consent still stands. This also gives the interviewer an opportunity to reiterate the focus of the research. It is then of paramount importance that the interviewer asks the interviewee if it is alright to record the interview in the way they intend. One way of collecting data from interviews is to write notes as the interviewee talks, noting down main themes and key points, but this generally precludes the interviewer from capturing verbatim quotes which can be an important source of evidence within qualitative research projects. Therefore, it is now more common for researchers to record interviews using a digital voice recorder or mobile phone. This enables full transcripts to be created for the analysis and interpretation stage, but this is not without its own issues.

Researchers are responsible for the care of the interviewee, especially in terms of their anonymity and confidentiality. Therefore, when interviews have been recorded it is very important that the recordings are saved to a secure site, such as a password protected hard drive or an encrypted drive, to ensure that no one else has access to the raw data. Once the researcher knows that the files are safe in an encrypted location, any files on the mobile phone or digital voice recorder should be deleted to ensure that they can't be accessed by others.

The researcher will then transcribe the recording to produce a written script of the interview. This is a time-consuming process but it is important for two main reasons. Firstly, a written transcript can be coded for data analysis and interpretation (see Chapter 7); this, in turn, facilitates high quality engagement with the data. Secondly, and more importantly, the creation of a transcript means the researcher can send a record of the interview to the interviewee and ask them if they are happy that it represents an accurate and fair representation of their discussion. This ethical process also adds to the validity of the data.

Observations

Observation is a research approach with a long history, although it should not be confused with the more recent use of observation for teacher accountability. Observation can give a very rich and useful strand of data within research projects, but it needs to be carefully planned and executed. Observation is more often used alongside other data collection techniques than by itself, as it can help in triangulating other data streams gained from classroom-based research projects. Triangulation (explained in more detail in Chapter 5) is a process where data from different collection techniques are compared to ascertain if there are common features or themes. There are a number of different ways of categorising observations and consideration should be given as to which is the most appropriate within any particular context.

One way of considering alternative approaches to observation is to think about the way in which data is captured. The two main options are:

- *Structured observation*: This form of observation often makes use of a structured data collection sheet which allows the observer to 'count' the number of instances of particular processes that are under consideration. For example, classroom observation might focus on recording who replies to particular questions and how often they do so. This can uncover patterns within the classroom, such as where people sit who are more involved in discussions: are they distributed across the classroom, or does the teacher tend to only choose students from one zone? A famous example of structured observation within a classroom environment comes from Rowe (1986) who measured the response time students were given when answering questions asked by teachers. The study suggested that typical response times rarely exceeded 1.5 seconds, but that even just waiting for 3 seconds before taking a response led to longer and more accurate answers from students. Structured observations will often provide quantitative data which gives researchers an opportunity to compare data across a number of lessons – although one concern here is the degree to which activities can be analysed consistently, especially by different observers.

- *Unstructured observation*: This form of observation centres on an observer taking notes during the course of the activity being observed. As a consequence, the data that is collected tends to be predominantly qualitative in nature and perceptual in form. Such observations will normally be carried out with a particular focus in mind, often through the use of a set of questions which provide a framework for the notes. The captured data is, therefore, in the form of written reflections and impressions of what the observer has seen. This can be extremely useful if the focus is carefully considered and planned, but criticisms are sometimes made that it may lead to observer bias. The use of other data collection techniques can be valuable in helping to triangulate the data collected from unstructured observations to give the written account a greater degree of validity.

Another way of categorising observations is to consider the degree to which the observer interacts with those who are being observed. There are three key approaches:

- *Unobtrusive*: This is where the observer has no interaction with those being observed. They attempt to position themselves within an environment in such a way that their presence goes as unnoticed as possible. This can be very difficult at first but if observations within a particular context are completed over a period of time, the group being observed often becomes accustomed to the presence of the observer and hence their observations become less obtrusive.

- *Reactive*: In this approach to observation those being observed are informed of the observation and its focus, but direct contact is not positively sought between the observer and the group. However, there may be a degree of interaction if it is believed that this will aid in understanding the activities or processes being observed. For example, the observer may join a group of students who are working on an activity of interest and ask them about what they are doing as a way of improving the detail and accuracy of their notes.

- *Participant*: This approach is often used if the research takes place over a long period of time. Here, the observer is actually an active member of the group and serves two roles, the first being as a member of the group and the second as an observer of the activities taking place. Extensive use is made of field notes, where the researcher writes reflective accounts about what they have observed and their experiences within the group over time, which are separate from the observation itself.

  Participant observation is particularly used within ethnographic studies. Ethnography is a research methodology where the researcher becomes a member of the group, with whom they work over an extended period of time, sometimes even months or years. The philosophical basis of the approach is that by spending long periods of time immersed within the group, a 'thick description' of the environment, groups and their processes can be captured and analysed. An example of how this might operate within the classroom would be for the observer to act as a teaching assistant, whilst at the same time researching a particular issue within the classroom. However, this obviously begins to present ethical concerns over issues such as informed consent, plus the research can take a long time to complete.

When considering the different approaches to observation sketched out above, it is obvious that it needs very careful planning. This includes the introduction of the observer to the group, their role within the environment, decisions about the focus for data collection and the media used for data capture and analysis/interpretation. Where structured observations are used, the researcher needs to consider the type and format of data to be captured.

Restrictions also need to be carefully considered. As suggested above, the introduction of an individual into a classroom can alter the dynamics of the group. Such disruption can diminish over time, as the group being observed becomes used to the observer, but this must always be kept in mind as any data analysis/interpretation moves forward. In addition, ethical issues need to be taken into consideration, including informed consent, anonymity and confidentiality, but also in terms of the ways in which data is captured during the course of the observation. Video can be extremely useful in allowing the observer to revisit the notes they have made during an observation, but obviously there are issues to consider such as child protection and consent.

Finally, observations, particularly those which are unstructured or of a participant approach, can be very partial in nature – observation notes or field notes provide a personal perspective on the activity and group being observed. This is why observations can be at their most useful when triangulated against other sources of data, rather than being used alone. However, if these constraints are taken into account, observation can be very valuable in helping researchers to understand and reflect on the particular activity or process under investigation.

Visual methods

Visual methods are a more recent approach in educational research. They cover a wide range of potential activities and can be useful in a number of ways, including affording stimuli for other data collection techniques such as interviewing and providing a useful medium for more participatory approaches to research. Whilst this area of data collection has developed only recently, it nevertheless has an extensive research literature, so what follows only touches the surface of some of the possibilities in this area.

Drawings

Drawings can be used to help capture people's perceptions or views on a wide range of topics. Asking participants to draw their understanding of a particular issue can allow them to communicate a depth and range of ideas which is not always possible in written form, particularly where the respondents are younger or have limited written literacy skills. One example of a study that used drawings to great effect considered children's perceptions of scientists. Samaras, Bonoti and Christidou (2012) asked 110 9–11-year-old Greek boys and girls to draw 'a scientist in his/her workplace'. A sample of 30 children were then interviewed using a semi-structured format. The drawings showed a generally stereotypical view of scientists, but from the interviews a more positive and less stereotypical view emerged. The drawings acted as a positive stimulus for discussion which would have probably been far less detailed had the interviews been used alone.

Photographs

As with drawings, photographs can act as a useful basis for developing a focus for interviews. Giving participants a camera and asking them to take pictures of particular locations – for example, locations within a school environment where they feel vulnerable or feel safe – can then be used as a starting point for investigation into issues relating to those locations. Once the photographs have been printed, they can then be stuck into sketchbooks and annotated by the participants. This can be followed by a discussion considering both the issues as they are at present and how they might be improved in the future.

Participatory video

With the increasingly ready availability of videoing equipment, such as on mobile phones, it is now possible to ask participants to create videos on a particular topic. The advantage of this type of approach is that it not only allows participants to capture visual footage, but it also enables them to create narrations linked to the visual data as it is being collected. The videos can be journalistic, reflective or even semi-fictitious, where individuals or groups may be asked to dramatise particular issues around the focus of the research. The resulting videos can be rich sources of data, which could then be used as the starting point for stimulated recall interviews or as a way of developing in-depth perspectives or clarifying the issues addressed.

In all of the above cases, it is important to consider the ethical issues carefully. Participants, especially children, tend to have a greater degree of freedom in deciding on the focus of data collection than is the case when using other data collection techniques. This leads to participants being at the centre of decisions concerning the evidence they capture. There is always a balancing act between giving children a voice within the research process and being alert to the potential for uncovering underlying child protection issues. This is why full consideration needs to be given to the way in which the research is conducted and the instructions shared with participants. Nevertheless, visual data collection can offer an extremely rich vein of insights and understanding and is a very positive and useful strand within educational research.

The best way of becoming proficient in carrying out the practical aspects of research is to spend sufficient time understanding and planning your data collection before undertaking the work. True proficiency then comes from using the data collected, each time reflecting on what has gone well and what hasn't. For this reason, it can be extremely useful to keep a research diary over the course of the research project, so that thoughts, problems and successes can all be recorded and used as part of a reflective process. In addition, where problems have occurred with data collection, it is important to be transparent in reporting such difficulties in any written account.

Summary

In Chapter 5 we outlined some basic methodological frameworks for carrying out research. In this chapter we have discussed some of the most common approaches used to collect data, as well as some of the basics concerning approaches to sampling. Data capture makes use of a wide variety of techniques, and here we have summarised a set of common methodologies and described some of the core features and issues to consider when attempting to develop high quality data collection.

Chapter 7
Thinking about data

Introduction

In this chapter we will consider two main aspects involved in thinking about data. Firstly, we outline some ideas concerning validity and generalisability. These are important considerations: if we are to make sense of and understand the world around us, we need to think about how we can ensure that the data we collect is valid and trustworthy. Associated with validity is the degree to which the data reported in research can be considered to be generalisable (i.e. the degree to which results can translate to multiple contexts). Secondly, we will give a brief introduction to some basic ways in which data can be systematically analysed to help researchers draw out patterns and explanations from the data they have collected. What we offer here is a simple introduction to enable those new to research to begin to understand some of the approaches and frameworks used when thinking about data.

Validity and reliability

Validity is defined by Wellington (2000: 201) as 'the degree to which a method, a test or research tool actually measures what it is supposed to measure'. Therefore, validity focuses on the extent to which methods can be seen as dependable and accurate within the context of the research in which they are used. We need to think about validity in terms of how the claims made within a piece of research are linked to the research methods used. As we have already discussed, there are a number of different research traditions within education, and as a consequence validity has been understood in a range of ways with regard to the link between claims and methods. As with much in research methods, there is a whole host of different ways to analyse the validity of a study and the examples offered here represent only a selection of some of the more common approaches.

Research which takes a predominantly positivist approach – often associated with larger scale quantitative research projects – uses a number of specific validity claims, including external and internal validity. Internal validity focuses on the relationship between observed variables. If a research project only attempts to demonstrate the degree of correlation between two variables then internal validity is not necessarily an issue. However, where claims about cause and effect are made then internal validity becomes important. Factors which may lead to validity problems include issues of temporality – that is, the cause must unambiguously precede the effect. If this cannot be established then the causal relationship becomes ambiguous at best. Observational effects can also be important, as the act of observing may itself change the phenomenon which is being measured. Finally, there may be issues around the groups used in the research, including issues of selection; if there is no true random assigning of individuals to experimental and control groups then outcomes may not be truly comparable. In addition, individuals or groups who drop out during a study can likewise alter the true random and comparable nature of the groups, which again calls into question the validity of the study. These validity problems are inherently linked to causal research, such as experiments and randomised control trials.

External validity is essentially a different way of considering the notion of generalisability. Here, consideration is given to the degree to which the results of the research can be generalised beyond the specific context in which it took place. If the research is replicated elsewhere, or is a replication study in its own right producing results similar to (or the same as) those gained elsewhere, this adds to the external validity of the research process and the results. However, within an educational context it is extremely difficult to replicate studies to any great degree due to the dynamic and often complex characteristics of the processes being researched.

When designing experimental research it is important to take these issues into account to ensure that the research is as valid as possible, and where issues do arise (e.g. groups dropping out of the research during the intervention) such shortcomings should be fully reported. Therefore, when reading experimental or randomised control trial reports, the reader should always keep in mind issues relating to validity when considering the degree to which they are able to trust the results and conclusions presented.

Internal and external validity are related to the issues of sampling and quantitative analysis. Obviously, this form of scrutiny does not translate into smaller scale qualitative research studies, so a number of different validity tools have been developed to analyse and demonstrate the link between the research process and the findings. The emphasis here is more on issues of credibility, trustworthiness and honest reporting. Since a lot of qualitative research is small scale and contextualised, cumulative validity tends to be used. This focuses on the outcomes of a piece of research in comparison to other similar pieces of research to ascertain whether the patterns and factors demonstrate similarities. One approach which has recently been developed to aid in this form of systematic meta-level analysis is 'qualitative research synthesis' (Major and Savin-Baden, 2010), which centres on detailed scrutiny across a number of qualitative studies to synthesise and generalise within a given area of research interest. Such approaches can lead to a greater level of trustworthiness within the research under consideration, and hence can result in a greater level of credibility.

Credibility can also be strengthened through a process known as communicative validity. Here, qualitative researchers will send interview transcripts to participants to ensure they are happy that they are an accurate representation of the discussion. Also, where possible, completed research reports will also be sent to participants so that they are able to comment on the degree to which they feel their own views have been accurately reflected. By communicating with participants in this way, researchers have a greater chance of ensuring that their reporting accurately reflects the opinions of those involved.

Validity is also linked to the notion of reliability. Reliability focuses on the degree to which any particular research approach could be used by other independent researchers and still gain the same results. However, this issue can be problematic as it assumes that the same results can always be obtained by applying the same methodology. Whilst it would be hoped that this is the case in closely controlled experimental settings, the complexity and idiosyncrasy of educational contexts may mean that results will naturally differ. It is particularly problematic in smaller scale research where it is the specific context (or unique elements within that context) which is the reason for conducting the research. There-fore, it is not unexpected that results will vary between contexts. This is one of the potential problems with the argument that the replication of results within educational research is the 'gold standard'. Classrooms are not laboratories. Reliability is still important, but it should centre on the research process rather than the results gained. In other words, reliability focuses on the degree to which the research methods used in a project are reported explicitly and transparently, and the extent to which this reporting would enable another group to reliably use the same set of tools. Therefore, replication in educational research is more likely to be about accurately using a research design rather than producing identical results.

Issues of validity and reliability should always be present in the reader's mind as they engage with any research they read or, indeed, when creat-ing their own small-scale research. Reporting should always make clear where issues have occurred which may impact on the validity and/or reliability of the research.

Analysing data

In the remainder of this chapter, we introduce some basic approaches to analysing data. This is in many ways the most difficult part of carry-ing out research as it is here that the researcher needs to make decisions concerning the 'narrative' which will emerge from the collected data. In small-scale research it is often relatively easy to collect the data; the really hard work is in the analysis and interpretation of that data. We will split the process into some basic approaches to the analysis of quantitative data and then qualitative data.

Quantitative data analysis

Quantitative data analysis generally relies on statistically based techniques. These include a full spectrum of approaches from relatively simple descriptive statistics to very complex multivariate statistical manipulations. Here, we outline some of the basic issues involved before signposting you to other materials which can help in developing your work in this area.

Types of quantitative data

If you look back at Table 6.1 (p. 92), you will see that the various question types used within questionnaires are identified as being one of four types of data – nominal, ordinal, interval or ratio. These categories characterise different types of variable (i.e. different types of data). It is important that the category of data being used is correctly identified as this has a significant bearing on the types of statistical manipulation which can be used when analysing the data.

Nominal scales are used for labelling variables such as gender or yes/no questions. There is little statistical manipulation that can be done with this type of data, but it is often important in terms of identifying subgroups within a sample or as background demographic information to help characterise the context of a research project.

Ordinal data is characterised by the significance of the order in the data, rather than the difference between the values. For example, you might ask a group of teachers how useful they found a training session on a scale of 1 (poor) to 5 (excellent). A score of 5 means that the training was better than a score of 4, and that in turn is better than a score of 3. However, the difference between 4 and 3 may be less than the difference between 4 and 5, as some individuals will rarely give a top mark because their assumption is that there can always be improvement. Therefore, the value simply expresses an order and does not necessarily indicate a consistent, differential scale. This is why rating scales provide ordinal data – an important point when considering the potential for the statistical manipulations below.

Interval data is any data where the difference between two values does have meaning – for example, the difference in height between 110 cm and 100 cm is the same as between 60 cm and 50 cm.

Ratio data has the same properties as interval data, but in addition it has a clear definition of zero – meaning that none of that variable can exist. Examination marks provide a good example of ratio data as it is possible for an individual to gain zero within an examination.

Different types of data allow for different descriptive statistics to be used when analysing, describing and interpreting quantitative data. Often, data will be analysed to get some notion of an average, or central tendency, as well as the degree to which the data is spread out from that average. A brief summary of the relationship between data type and simple descriptive statistical manipulations appears in Table 7.1.

	Nominal	**Ordinal**	**Interval**	**Ratio**
Frequency distribution	X	X	X	X
Median, interquartile range		X	X	X
Mean, standard deviation			X	X

Table 7.1. The relationship between data types and simple statistical manipulation.

The table shows that the type of data produced impacts on the statistical manipulation that is possible (expanded in the worked example below). Nominal data allows for little more than the calculation of frequency distribution (i.e. how often any one particular category is chosen). This means that nominal data can give some idea of central tendency through identification of the mode (i.e. the category which is most frequently chosen). Ordinal data also allows for frequency distributions to be calculated, but in addition it allows for the calculation of the median value as a measure of central tendency. It can also give some idea of the spread of the data through the calculation of the interquartile range.

Interval and ratio data can be manipulated in the same way as nominal and ordinal data to give frequency distributions and median/interquartile range data. However, these types of data provide mean (calculation of central tendency or average) and standard deviation (calculation of spread) values, which are much more accurate in defining central tendency and spread in datasets than is the case for medians and interquartile ranges. Below, we provide a worked example of simple descriptive statistical calculations relating to different types of data and statistical techniques.

One debate surrounding statistical calculations which you may come across relates to the characterisation of rating scale data. In Chapter 6, rating scales were identified as providing ordinal data. However, there is ongoing discussion as to whether or not the value differences between steps on a rating scale are consistent. In the example given above concerning the quality of a training session, some would argue that there is a consistent interval between the values 1 to 5, whilst others would argue that this is not the case. This is important as some research presents simple descriptive statistics relating to rating scales using the mean and standard deviation. This can only be done if the assumption is that the intervals between the points on the rating scale are in some way equidistant. However, given that we cannot be sure that all respondents understand and experience the scale in this way, we believe that rating scales should be analysed as ordinal data, and therefore should only present median and interquartile range data.

The introduction to quantitative data analysis given here only covers some of the most basic statistical manipulations which can be carried out on quantitative data, particularly from questionnaires. If this is an area of interest which you would like to develop, it is important that you spend time understanding both data collection techniques and the associated statistical techniques in detail, which is beyond the scope of this book. However, if you look at the annotated bibliography in Appendix 1, there are one or two suggestions for books which cover more complex statistical techniques, such as univariate and multivariate inferential statistics, which will help you begin to develop a more detailed understanding of this area of quantitative research.

Worked example of some basic descriptive statistics

Table 7.2 illustrates part of a hypothetical dataset tracking student characteristics, perceptions of their learning and attainment across three course modules. The first step in analysing this type of data is to identify, for each column, what type of data is being presented.

Gender and course

The data collected for gender and course (see Table 7.3) are nominal data as the choices made by respondents are related to choosing a category. Therefore, analysis of this data allows for the creation of frequency distributions. In this case, this involves counting up the number of males and females who have responded to the questionnaire, plus the number on each course, resulting in the following simple analysis.

Females	9		Business	5
Males	6		Education	3
			English	7

Table 7.3. Summary data for gender and course followed.

However, in terms of simple descriptive statistics, this is as much as we are able to do in analysing the data produced.

Perceptions about learning and the course

The next three columns of data have all been captured using a rating scale. Therefore, this data is ordinal and, as such, it can provide frequency distribution data. It also allows for the use of median and interquartile range calculations to identify both a central tendency, or average, from the data as well as the degree of spread.

Gender	Course	I am confident about my learning	I enjoy my course	My tutors make learning interesting	Mark (%)		
		1 – Strongly agree 2 – Agree 3 – Neither agree nor disagree 4 – Disagree 5 – Strongly disagree			Module 1	Module 2	Module 3
Male	Business	2	2	2	53	68	53
Female	English	1	2	2	65	54	86
Female	Education	3	1	1	76	70	66
Male	English	4	2	4	52	51	56
Female	English	2	3	3	73	65	73
Female	Business	3	1	2	48	81	43
Male	Business	1	4	5	68	72	64
Male	English	1	2	1	79	62	49
Female	English	5	3	3	73	78	74
Male	Education	3	2	2	51	50	54
Female	English	2	5	4	65	62	79

Continued

115

| Gender | Course | 1 – Strongly agree 2 – Agree 3 – Neither agree nor disagree 4 – Disagree 5 – Strongly disagree | | | Mark (%) | | |
		I am confident about my learning	I enjoy my course	My tutors make learning interesting	Module 1	Module 2	Module 3
Male	Business	4	1	2	82	73	71
Female	Education	1	3	1	62	67	58
Female	English	2	4	1	72	59	69
Female	Business	3	2	2	42	69	46

Table 7.2. Sample dataset tracking student characteristics, perceptions of learning and assessment data.

To calculate the median, the data needs to be presented in order from the lowest to the highest value. For the question which asks how confident students are in their learning, this would result in the following line of numbers:

1 1 1 1 2 2 2 2 3 3 3 3 4 4 5

The median value is simply the middle value within the dataset. Because there are 15 numbers, the median value is the eighth value in the line (identified by the arrow). If there had been 14 numbers in the dataset then the median point would fall between the seventh and eighth numbers. Therefore, to calculate the median value where the dataset has an even number of values, the two numbers on either side of the midpoint are added together and divided by 2. In this particular example, the median value is 2.

To understand how spread out the dataset is there are two potential measures. The first is the range, which is simply the difference between the values of the lowest and highest numbers in the dataset. Therefore, the range in this example is $5 - 1 = 4$. If we imagine the line of data being split into four equal parts, then we can calculate the interquartile range (IQR) which is calculated using the middle 50% of the data points within the dataset. This is used to give some impression as to how narrowly or widely data is spread around the median. The bigger the value of the IQR, the more spread out the data is around the median.

Where the number of data points is an odd number, we can take the numbers on either side of the median (Q1 and Q3) and again find the middle number. Therefore, in this case, to calculate the interquartile range, the data is grouped in the following way:

1 1 1 1 2 2 2 2 3 3 3 3 4 4 5

Q1   Q3

In this dataset, Q1 equals 1 and Q3 equals 3. The interquartile range has the value of Q3 – Q1, which in this case is $3 - 1 = 2$. So, for this particular dataset the median value is 2 and the interquartile range is 2.

For these rating scale questions, the datasets provide the following statistics:

	Median	IQR
I am confident about my learning	2	2
I enjoy my course	2	1
My tutors make learning interesting	2	2

Table 7.4. Median and interquartile range statistics for learning perceptions.

These summary statistics show that the median is the same for all three questions, but that the responses are slightly more spread out in the first and third questions than for the second.

Attainment on modules

The final three columns in the dataset are summaries of attainment over three modules. These datasets are ratio data because it is possible to get zero on a test. Therefore, these datasets can be analysed using mean and standard deviation as measures of central tendency and the spread of the data. The mean is calculated by adding all the values and dividing by the number of data points, so for module 1 the mean is found by the following calculation:

$$(53 + 65 + 76 + 52 + 73 + 48 + 68 + 79 + 73 + 51 + 65 + 82 + 62 + 72 + 42) / 15 = 64$$

Therefore, the mean of attainment in module 1 is 64%. If we want to get an idea of the degree of spread from this value then we can calculate the standard deviation. This is a measure of dispersion – the larger the number indicating a greater spread of scores away from the mean.

To find the standard deviation we start by calculating how far from the mean each score is:

Score	42	48	51	52	53	62	65	65
Deviation from mean	-22	-16	-13	-12	-11	-2	1	1
Score	68	72	73	73	76	79	82	
Deviation from mean	4	8	9	9	12	15	18	

Table 7.5. Deviation of each value from the mean.

The deviation scores are then squared:

Score	42	48	51	52	53	62	65	65
(Deviation from mean)^2	484	256	169	144	121	4	1	1
Score	68	72	73	73	76	79	82	
(Deviation from mean)^2	16	64	81	81	144	225	324	

Table 7.6. Squared deviation of each value from the mean.

The sum of these values is then divided by the sample size to give the variance (or the average squared deviation of the sample) – here calculated as: 2115 / 15 = 141.

The standard deviation is then the square root of the variance value, i.e. $\sqrt{141} = 11.9$.

This means that the data can be summarised as having a mean value of 64% with a standard deviation of 11.9%. The larger the standard deviation, the more spread out the data in the dataset.

The statistical output for the three modules is:

Module	Mean	Standard deviation
1	64.0%	11.9%
2	65.4%	8.9%
3	62.7%	12.3%

Table 7.7. Mean and standard deviation scores for modules 1 to 3.

These summary statistics show that the three modules have roughly equal mean scores, but that module 2 has less of a spread of marks than modules 1 or 3.

All of the calculations above can be carried out using free online calculators or within standard computer spreadsheet packages, but a useful rule of thumb to consider when using any statistical approach is to use them only if you have a generally good understanding of how they are calculated and what they mean. Using statistical packages by following instructions blindly without really getting to grips with statistical understanding can lead to spurious calculations and data.

Qualitative data analysis

Much, but not all, qualitative data in small-scale research relates to the use of text, particularly interview transcripts. Here, we show how interview data is analysed in an attempt to draw out themes in a way that makes the analysis and subsequent interpretation valid and reliable. Qualitative research, whilst often small scale, requires a large amount of time to make sense of the data collected. As discussed in Chapter 4, any attempt to cherry-pick particular comments or perspectives from the data to prove a predetermined point is to act unethically within the research process. Transcription and coding of data are essential steps in ensuring a valid and representative interpretation of the data collected.

Below is an example of thematic coding, one of a number of different approaches to making sense of the large quantity of data that is captured through the use of interviewing. This coding approach relies on identifying themes within the literature as a framework for analysing and understanding the data which has been captured. An alternative approach, which identifies themes within the data without recourse to the literature, is known as emergent coding. It involves categorising themes within the data as they emerge from the transcripts. However, for this approach to be successful, the researcher needs to read through the transcripts multiple times to ensure that the codes are coherent and reflect the actual content of the transcripts.

A further way of ensuring validity with any form of coding approach is for more than one researcher to read through the transcripts, apply thematic codes or create emergent codes, before comparing their work with another researcher who has completed the same task independently. This allows for comparison and discussion about the coding frameworks which have been created.

Thematic coding of qualitative data

If your research involves collecting qualitative data, you will need to build into your research design a systematic way of organising and analysing the data. In this section we look at how you might use thematic coding, using a manual method, to help you organise and categorise the data so that you can interpret and make sense of it.

Drawing themes from the literature

A thorough literature review can inform your research questions as well as, for example, the questions you ask in a semi-structured interview. It can also help you to pre-empt some of the themes you will use to organise and categorise your interview data. So, a literature search on factors affecting female teachers' career progression might generate themes that include:

- Family and caring responsibilities
- Institutional sexism

- Mentoring

- Networking

- Access to professional development opportunities

- Sources of job satisfaction.

You might use these themes as the basis for the core questions you would ask in the interview. Of course, in a semi-structured interview you will also allow participants to discuss issues that are not reflected in the literature you have reviewed but which are important to them. This means that some themes you did not anticipate might also emerge from the data. This is one of the strengths of semi-structured interviewing. By building an interview around questions drawn from the literature, together with some open-ended questions and probing, this method offers scope to compare your data with what you already know from the literature, as well as to harness your participants' unique experiences and perceptions. It allows for comparison, but it also allows participants to define for themselves what has been influential in their experience.

So, as well as asking the participants to talk about their perceptions of how family, sexism, mentoring, networking, professional development and job satisfaction have influenced their career decisions, you might also ask, 'Have there been other experiences that have had an impact on your career decisions?' This then allows you to draw out a fuller narrative and helps you to understand individuals' experiences and perceptions, without limiting them to a researcher-defined agenda. Your list of themes is likely to grow as you add in topics that emerge from participants' narratives. So, your final list might include:

- Family and caring responsibilities

- Institutional sexism

- Mentoring

- Networking

- Access to professional development opportunities

- Sources of job satisfaction

- Marriage and relationships

- Health

- Professional and personal values

- Career planning

- Love of the subject

- Love of classroom teaching

- Importance of positive relationships with colleagues

- A strong emphasis on pupil welfare and achievement.

Having identified the themes, you are ready to systematically code your data. One way to do this is to accord each theme a colour, highlighting sections of the transcript in the appropriate colour. This can become complicated, however, as often a section of transcript will fall into more than one category, meaning that you need to use more than one colour to categorise a single extract. In some cases you can make a judgement about which seems to be the key theme, but it isn't always that straightforward and some decisions will need to be made about what is most important. By colour coding all parts of a transcript, you can create a visual representation showing the extent to which each theme was discussed by your participants and the extent to which your data are consonant with the issues identified in the literature.

Qualitative data analysis software is available (e.g. NVivo) to assist with the process of coding textual data. However, you will need to have a thorough understanding of the principles of coding and be very familiar with your data in order to use the software effectively. Whilst NVivo is very useful in that it allows you, for example, to pull out coded pieces of text and collect them together with other examples, it takes skill and understanding to do this well. We would recommend, at least in the early stages, coding the data manually. This process allows you to get to know the data very well and gain an in-depth understanding of each narrative. This can help you to avoid the potential pitfall of using electronic software to code data before you are fully familiar with it, which can result in the fragmentation of the narrative into bits and pieces of text which become de-contextualised and meaningless.

Having colour-coded evidence of the different themes in your transcripts, you then need to find a systematic way to compare these across the sample to ascertain which themes seem to be of importance to all or most of your participants, and which seem to be more idiosyncratic or applicable only to a small group within the sample. We suggested in Chapter 2 that it is helpful to draw up a matrix showing each theme you identify and indicate in which transcripts there was strong, some or no evidence of the theme. From this overview you will be able to establish with confidence what the key themes were for your sample. For example:

	Participants							
Themes	Jane	Jacky	Rajinder	Gail	Ingrid	Monica	Geeta	Total
Having children influenced career	2	2	2	0	1	0	2	9
Caring for elderly parents influenced career	0	0	1	2	2	0	0	5
Preference for classroom teaching	2	2	2	2	2	1	2	13
Limited to geographical area	2	2	2	2	2	1	1	12
Health issues	0	0	2	1	0	0	0	3

Table 7.8. Themes matrix for summarising data patterns.

From Table 7.8, you can see that a preference for classroom teaching, rather than leadership, influenced the career decisions of most women in the sample. It also indicates that for certain individuals, health issues have been very influential as career-shaping factors. Although there is only one woman for whom this was a major issue, her particular story may indicate that it has been key in framing her decisions in the last few years. In reporting your findings, you would need to find a way to report the most common themes whilst not losing the important idiosyncratic stories.

We provide below as a worked example an extract from an interview that formed a part of a study on women teachers' perceptions of the factors affecting their career decisions (Smith, 2007). You would use colour coding, although below we have used text formatting (which is slightly less clear), for which the key is:

- Marriage and relationship
- **Pastoral versus subject**
- **Opportunities to enact leadership**
- *Societal expectations of mothers*
- *Own education and socialisation*
- *Family responsibilities/having primary responsibility for childcare.*

Extract from interview with Coral

Could you tell me about your career to date and what you would say the major factors have been in shaping your career decisions.

I started off at School X, an 11–16, in 1975 ... I stayed there for three-and-a-half years, met my husband there, and **felt that I wanted to do some further A level and GCSE kind of work ... so I moved sideways, in fact ... And I was quite happy for a while, but then I think the pastoral side of things started to interest me and there was a bit of a clash between [the subject] and the pastoral side.** I think if I'd pursued the [subject] side of things, I could have become head of department fairly quickly. At the time, I think it would have upset my husband's and my relationship had I gone for head of department, really gone for a career at that point.

Did you have kids at that point?

No, we didn't actually. And we were both quite career minded, but I think if I'd gone ahead and sort of become a head of department ... But fortunately I had an opening in the pastoral field there and I went towards that, being an assistant year head ... And then when somebody went on maternity leave I ended up doing their job as division head ... division heads really played a massive part in running the school. They were like the four head teachers within the

school if you like, or deputies ... And I actually felt that I played quite a major role there, *and it was also a good thing because, two years previous to that I'd had my first child. At that time, they didn't really approve of mothers going back into school. I think only one person had done it before me, taken maternity leave and then gone back ... before that women left and brought their children up. So it was very much a new thing and I had to work twice as hard to prove I was half as good, and that's how I felt. But I achieved that,* **and I actually, by getting this division job, I felt that I'd achieved a lot, lot more ... I had a very good rapport with the children, all the other outside agencies, with the senior management – I felt I got on really well.**

What was it that led you to choose teaching as a career in the first place?

... I got involved in [subject] and realised I was quite good at [it]. I suppose I just felt I would like to teach others [my subject].

So it was your subject, really, in your case, that made you go for teaching?

Yes. But I think in many ways the high school ... that I was at ... there wasn't a lot of career guidance and you ended up just going for university or teacher training college. And then if you went to university you ended up doing a PGCE.

Was it a girls' grammar?

It was a girls' grammar, so basically those who could went into teaching ...

The expectation was that academic girls would go into teaching?

I think so, yes. It was very much that ... They didn't look and think, ah, you might be good at doing this ... Even at university we didn't get an awful lot of career guidance. It was very much, yes, well, you can go into teaching. What else can you do with your degree really?! And the degree was very much an old-fashioned type degree ... If I had my time again I think I would have done something completely different.

When you were at university, were you expected to go into teaching because you were female, or was it an expectation that everybody would go into teaching?

I think maybe, possibly a lot of the people I mixed with were thinking about teaching and they were the girls, whereas the boys hadn't really got any career ideas at that point. I don't think the boys actually thought about what they were going to do. They were just going to take the risk, whereas the girls had actually thought, oh well, I think I will do this when

I've finished. And, so, maybe the boys did end up going into teaching, I don't know ...

Have you ever experienced sexism or discrimination at work in any form?

Yes, when I had my first child at [school] I was told by the deputy head that I should be at home looking after my baby! That was when I was trying to make a career for myself, to prove that, you know, I was worthy of being employed and I wasn't just somebody who was there for pin money.

And that is relatively recent really, isn't it?

Not really. It was in 1984 ... It was just on the turning point, actually, when women were returning to work, taking maternity leave and maternity rights. Yes – I was so bad! Not because I was doing a bad job, he just felt that I should be at home with my children.

In what circumstances did he say that to you?

I think it was just during conversation, during the break. It was just chat. It wasn't because I was in his office because I couldn't cope with something. It was just sheer prejudice ... I mean he probably felt because his wife had looked after their children, that was the role of the mother, and that was his personal opinion. He was 10 years older. It wasn't anything to do with the fact that I was inadequate professionally. He felt free to say that!

Did you make any response to him?

No. I just took it and thought, well, I will have to prove ... Well, I did react, because it made me stronger. And it made me stronger to do quite a few ... I felt that the person that I was working alongside also wondered why I worked, and whilst he appreciated me professionally, I think he did feel that, you know, maybe I should be at home, looking after my children ...

Did you feel that you had to prove that it could be done, that you had your children and could hold down the job?

Yes. Yes. There was a certain amount of personal 'I'm going to do this'... I think we feel we've got to do everything to perfection – to work twice as hard to prove I was half as good, but that's in my mind, not necessarily in others' ...

Have your aspirations changed since you started teaching?

Yes ... I think when I first started teaching I was going to become a deputy head, possibly, and I was going to really get up the career ladder. And then I started to widen my horizons, and that stopped me going in one direction quickly. I sort of spread out. And then having a family just

puts a completely different perspective on things. You have to think of somebody else first before you can think of yourself.

Has family been the major thing really in shaping your career?

Yes. Yes. Yes. And also, once you actually get to do something you enjoy, you think, well, promotion is not that important. The role is important, the job is important if you enjoy it, but I think ultimately you are juggling. You are juggling the whole time. And I think you want a little bit of your career and a little bit of everything. There is no reason why you can't do a bit of each well ... I've never felt that I wanted to be that far away from the family, and I suppose that has also limited my career ... My husband works quite a long way away, on the other side of the city, so I've always felt that I would want to be within about 10 or 15 minutes of getting home in case there was a problem. And that has been at the back of my mind, that I would have to be the one that had to deal with it.

And has that always been the case when there has been a problem?

Yes, it has actually. And it shouldn't have been. I've obviously taken that role on myself ... I think some of it has been my own making. Maybe it's my own upbringing that my mother always sorted us out, my father never really had anything to do with the problems, but then she wasn't working. I have two roles, work and home; she had just one. But I think it's still instilled within you, you know, the good old [fashioned] upbringing, that mum, in fact runs the house ...

As is probably evident from this extract, some decisions need to be made by the researcher in terms of the themes and labels they will use to identify the main issues emerging from the interview. There are sections of this transcript where Coral talks about, for example, the attitude of certain colleagues to her when she returned to work having had children. We could have coded this as 'societal expectations of mothers', but it might equally have been labelled 'experiences of sexism' or 'impact of family on career'. It is important to be consistent in the use of labelling if comparison across the sample is to be possible.

Summary

In this chapter we have introduced some of the basic techniques to use for analysing and making sense of the data we have collected. Good quality analysis is crucial to providing valid explanations and interpretations of data, and it should not be rushed. Trying to complete this element of a research project quickly can lead to inaccuracies or biases in your interpretation, which will affect the utility of the research. If you choose to write a research report summarising your research, you should also describe how you completed the analysis of your data.

Chapter 8

Developing
small-scale research

Introduction

Conducting research well is a difficult process, but it can also be extremely rewarding. When you begin to think about carrying out research for the first time it is often an intimidating prospect as it generally appears that those carrying out research appear to do so with few problems, particularly as the research methods sections within academic papers are suggestive of a process that is smooth and meets very few issues or troubles along the way. This is rarely the case, however, and most research projects will at some point run into problems, be they large or small. Therefore, the best way of becoming a proficient researcher is simply to take the plunge and begin to develop small-scale studies.

It is important that any project, however small scale, is well planned and conducted in a measured and reflective way. High quality research does not happen rapidly or unthinkingly, with the sole intent of capturing a body of data as quickly as possible in an attempt to prove a predetermined point. To retain the integrity of the project, each step needs to be carefully considered and planned in advance, and reflected upon whilst being undertaken, so that any issues or problems can be resolved.

Figure 8.1 is a simple flow diagram which outlines the basic stages of a small-scale research project.

As we outlined in Chapter 4, the reasons for doing a research project can vary widely, so the first part of any project should begin by identifying the problem or issue of interest. Sufficient time should be spent at this stage reflecting upon the main focus. To move from a general notion to a specific idea is not always easy, but research tends to be simpler to plan and execute if the focus is well defined and manageable. Therefore, an initial period considering the key points, perhaps alongside informal discussion with others, can help to sharpen your ideas. It is also important to emphasise that research does not necessarily have to look

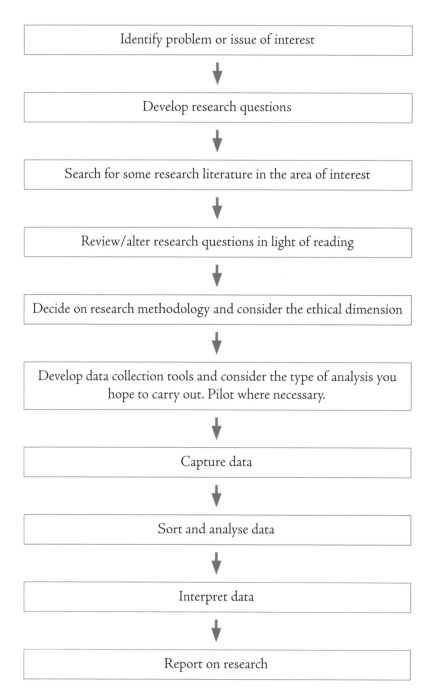

Figure 8.1. Simple project process flow diagram.

at a problem. It can be used for a multitude of other reasons, including exploring a new area of study, evaluating a new intervention or capturing the characteristics of an already successful process.

Once the problem or issue has been clearly defined, a number of research questions should then be formulated (as outlined in Chapter 4). Research questions are particularly important in terms of giving the project coherence. They help to direct any interaction with the literature and are crucial in deciding the methodological approach. The research questions also inform the selection of data collection tools – for example, they will play a role in the generation of questionnaire or interview questions. In interpreting data and reporting on the research a key consideration for the researcher(s) is the extent to which the research questions have or haven't been answered. Therefore, time should be given over to this process to ensure the research questions are clear and do actually throw light upon the issue or problem of interest.

The research questions also act as the starting point for deciding on any literature that will be read as a background to the project. A lot of research literature is held behind pay walls, so for the researcher without access to an electronic library and online search facilities it is not always easily available. However, there are an increasing number of open access journals and final draft versions of papers which are freely available online. Once a number of papers have been identified, they should be read critically (see Chapter 3) and assessed for their utility in helping to inform the emerging project. They might offer useful evidence, methodological insights which can be incorporated into plans for the project and may even suggest new questions about the area to which they have no answer. After spending time engaging with some of the research literature, it can be useful to return to your research questions to see if you wish to modify them in light of your reading.

With some background knowledge and the research questions in place, the next big decision is to decide on the type of methodology you wish to use for your research project. Those outlined in Chapter 5 are some of the most commonly used methodologies, so you need to consider which would be most appropriate in helping you to answer your research questions. For example, if you wish to trial a new pedagogic intervention you may decide to use either an experimental approach or an action research approach. The choice may depend on the type of analysis and interpretation you feel is most appropriate and also the approach that you feel most comfortable with. It may even be the case that you wish to carry out research over an extended period of time and decide to use a two-phase approach, with phase 1 making use of action research to begin to understand and develop an intervention, followed by a second phase which then tests the overall impact of the final intervention using an experimental approach. Whatever methodology you choose, you need to think carefully about how it will enable you to answer your research questions and the degree to which it can be practically realised within your own context.

As you begin thinking about which methodology you intend to use, you should also consider any ethical issues which may be applicable. For example, beyond the central concerns of anonymity, confidentiality and informed consent, are you intending to engage with any vulnerable groups? Is your research focused on an area of work which may be deemed controversial or sensitive? These are not reasons to halt the research, but careful consideration needs to be given as to how the research can be carried out without exposing groups or individuals, including yourself, to harm. Once these ethical dimensions have been considered, they then need to be embedded within the remaining process, rather than being deemed to have been solved and thus no longer of any importance.

Once the methodological framework has been determined, decisions need to be made concerning the sample (see Chapter 6), followed by the major decision concerning which data collection tools will be used. The main data collection tools are outlined in Chapter 6 – these will provide a framework for developing simple small-scale research. As with all other stages in the process, it is important that time is given to reflecting on the content of the tools and how they will be used. For example, the research questions should provide an important initial framework for any questionnaire or interview questions, and equally they can be the starting point for any observation frameworks that are developed for the project. However, where possible, the best way of measuring the potential utility of the tools created is to test them out in small-scale piloting. The quality of the final tools will be much better if this process can be undertaken. When developing data collection tools, also keep in mind the multitude of potential biases (see Chapters 2 and 4) and the need to reflect on the validity of the framework being developed (see Chapter 7) to ensure that the quality of the data collected is as high as possible.

Once data collection tools have been developed and piloted, they can then be used to capture the data for the project. Again, it is important to consider the ethical questions that you identified earlier and ensure that this collection period is completed in as principled a manner as possible. This includes careful handling of the data to make sure that it remains confidential and is not accessible to others.

Once collected, the data then needs to be sorted. This may include downloading data from an online survey tool into a database for analysis, the tallying of questionnaire data if collected physically or the transcribing of audio files from interviews in preparation for coding. This element of the project can be time consuming, particularly where interview transcriptions are concerned. However, the quality of analysis is extremely important and therefore coding is a crucial step in getting to grips with the data. Merely listening to audio files and noting down points which are deemed important can lead to an inaccurate and biased assessment of the data.

Having sorted the research data, the next phase is analysis (see Chapter 7) which may include the statistical analysis of numeric data, coding and so on. From this you can begin to identify emerging patterns within the data, which will serve as the basis for answering the research questions asked at the start of the project. Data interpretation is obviously a crucial element within the research project and, again, requires time. Patterns which emerge from numeric analysis, interview transcripts or observation frameworks are central to the interpretation of the data gathered. These patterns are the backbone of any analysis and discussion of the research data, and therefore need to be clearly evidenced from the information that has been collected.

Interpretation should be developed in relation to the initial research questions. It may be that these questions have been answered in the positive or the negative, they may have been only partially answered or, indeed, the data may demonstrate patterns or issues which are not covered by the research questions at all. Your analysis should attempt to answer the research questions, but also highlight and emphasise those areas which are of interest but not covered by the original questions. In addition, it is important not to 'hunt' for the 'correct' answer. Negative results can be as useful as positive ones, and finding out that an intervention hasn't worked can be extremely valuable, particularly if the reasons for its failure can begin to be understood. It is from these interpretations that any conclusions or initial insights can begin to be drawn.

The final element within a research project is reporting. This can take many forms and can range from the informal to the formal. Oral presentations, posters and short reports are all possibilities. However, any writing that is produced needs to be carefully considered and critical (see Chapter 3), and the methodological aspects of the project should be made clear so that those engaging with it are able to determine the degree to which the interpretation given is in keeping with the approach taken. In addition, good reporting will often conclude with further questions or issues which could usefully be considered in future research projects, as well as potential implications of the work for policy and practice.

The outline given above is intended to help those wanting to carry out a small-scale research project, particularly how the various aspects of a research project might fit together. Reiterating the points made at the start of the chapter, the only way to become a proficient researcher is to conduct small-scale research projects, reflecting on and learning from the processes as you carry them out. No research project is perfect, and the execution of all research projects involves problems and restrictions, particularly as most educational research occurs in natural settings which can't be highly controlled. As well as developing research proficiency through undertaking and reflecting on the practice of research, engaging with the research methods literature can also help develop knowledge and conceptual understanding as a basis for developing practice. Therefore, in Appendix 1 we provide a short annotated bibliography of some of the research methods publications which you can engage with to help develop, extend and deepen your understanding of this area.

Summary

This chapter has given suggestions for an approach to developing small-scale research projects and should be used in conjunction with the other chapters in the book. Our aim in this book has been to give an overview and a practical introduction to the huge range of possible research approaches available in educational research in the hope that these insights will ignite readers' interest in understanding and conducting their own research. As you try out some of the ideas described here, and begin to develop your own research literacy, we wish you luck and hope you gain satisfaction through interacting with the process of research.

Appendix 1

Developing your understanding of research methods – suggested further reading

Arthur, J., Waring, M., Coe, R. and Hedges, L. V. (2012) *Research Methods and Methodologies in Education* (London: SAGE).

This book provides a wide-ranging overview of research methods in education, including sections on conducting research, research design and data collection. It has some particularly useful chapters on statistical analysis, including multiple linear regression, multilevel analysis and effect sizes, written by leading academics in their respective fields.

Campbell, A. and Groundwater-Smith, S. (2007) *An Ethical Approach to Practitioner Research* (Abingdon: Routledge).

This book provides an in-depth discussion of the ethical issues which need to be considered when developing practitioner research. It moves well beyond the 'legalistic' aspects of confidentiality, anonymity and informed consent, and begins to consider the deeper issues of professional values, relationships and the complexity of working as both researcher and practitioner.

Daniel, J. (2012) *Sampling Essentials: Practical Guidelines for Making Sampling Choices* (London: SAGE).

Sampling is a crucial element in developing a coherent research design, and this book looks in detail at the wide variety of options available. It covers both nonprobability and probability sampling, and also considers sampling issues within mixed methods projects.

de Vaus, D. (2014) *Surveys in Social Research*, 6th edn (Abingdon: Routledge).

Surveys can be a very useful research tool, particularly when trying to characterise and identify a particular issue within a given context. This book not only considers the nature and underlying theory relating to surveys but also considers in detail approaches for constructing and completing questionnaires and how the data gained from a survey can be analysed. The fourth part of this book, extending to well over 100 pages, focuses on the use of statistical methods to interrogate quantitative data and is a very good introduction to statistics for those who are unsure or who lack confidence in this area.

Howell, K. E. (2013) *An Introduction to the Philosophy of Methodology* (London: SAGE).

The philosophical underpinnings of social research can often be confusing and seemingly esoteric. This book provides an interesting and clear introduction to many of the philosophical foundations within a wider social research context, considering aspects of theory, paradigms of enquiry and issues concerning reliability and validity. It is a very useful introduction to this area of research methods.

McAteer, M. (2013) *Action Research in Education* (London: SAGE).

This is a very practical book which begins by outlining the nature of action research, including some idea of its complexity, before moving on to a more detailed consideration of how to undertake action research projects. It is a useful first book for those who wish to develop their understanding and practice in this area of methodology.

Newby, P. (2010) *Research Methods for Education* (Harlow: Pearson Education).

This book offers a comprehensive consideration of research methods within education. It covers all aspects of the research design process and does so in detail. It is clearly explained and presented throughout, and offers an excellent reference guide for those who have some knowledge of research methods already and want to extend both their understanding and practice in this area.

O'Dwyer, L. M. and Bernauer, J. A. (2014) *Quantitative Research for the Qualitative Researcher* (London: SAGE).

For those who have started to develop their understanding of research by conducting mainly small-scale qualitative research, this book provides an excellent introduction to the development and execution of quantitatively based research. It considers issues relating to sampling, validity and generalisability, research design and statistically based analysis, attempting to explain and provide support for those who have little grounding in quantitative approaches.

Saldana, J. (2009) *The Coding Manual for Qualitative Researchers* (London: SAGE).

The use of coding is central to the analysis of a lot of qualitative data. This book offers a short introduction to the process of coding before describing and exemplifying a host of different approaches to coding data. It is an extremely useful reference guide for those involved in qualitative data analysis.

Silverman, D. (2011) *Interpreting Qualitative Data*, 4th edn (London: SAGE).

Qualitative research offers a wide range of potential approaches to data collection and analysis. This book provides a detailed insight into many of the main approaches to qualitative research including interviewing, the analysis of text and the use of visual images. It also discusses issues relevant to conducting credible, valid research, and is therefore an extremely useful reference guide for those wanting to further develop their understanding and practice within qualitative research.

Thomas, G. (2009) *How To Do Your Research Project: A Guide for Students in Education and Applied Social Sciences* (London: SAGE).

As the title suggests, this book has been written to give a clear and detailed consideration of the steps involved in developing and carrying out a research project. For those who have started to engage with the process of small-scale research, this is an extremely useful book to extend and develop your work as a practitioner researcher.

Townsend, A. (2012) *Action Research: The Challenges of Understanding and Changing Practice* (Maidenhead: Open University Press).

This introduction to action research is both clear and critical, with a detailed consideration of the underpinning and foundations of action research, together with useful practical information on developing action research projects. For those interested in developing both their understanding and their capacity to carry out high quality action research, this is an excellent book.

Appendix 2
Exemplar research ethics consent form

Dear Student,

Research methods research

Phil Wood and Joan Smith are exploring the development of new learning approaches to research methods at master's level. We would like to capture your experiences and learning as we move through the module over the course of the year. The project will involve the collection of a number of datasets:

- Collaborative preparation, observation and evaluation of four research sessions in research methods.

- Digital voice recording of planning and evaluation meetings.

- Observation of the four research sessions.

- The collection of students' viewpoints, for which you will be asked to volunteer.

- Review interviews with researchers, for which you will be asked to volunteer.

- Filming (generic non-moving) of sessions in the module.

- Collection of concept maps and explanations at the end of each session.

- Periodic review questionnaires and focus groups.

- Analysis of module assignments and end-of-course dissertations.

Any information collected will be held in a secure place to ensure that the views of the participants remain anonymous, and will only be used by us to aid understanding of classroom learning and student development. Any reporting will only use collective data or anonymised quotes which cannot be attributed to individuals. If you do not wish to be included in the research, please do *not* fill in and return the slip below, although you should be aware that observations and filming of sessions will continue, but we will ensure that your participation is not included in any research analysis. If you do agree to being involved in the research project at this point in time, you can, of course, withdraw consent and exit from the process at any point.

If you have any further questions concerning this matter, please feel free to contact Phil Wood/Joan Smith.

✂ ....

I consent to taking part in 2014–15 research methods project for the MA International Education.

Name: ....

Your signature: .... Date: ....

References

Becker, H. S. (1986) *Writing for Social Scientists: How to Start and Finish Your Thesis* (Chicago, IL: University of Chicago Press).

Creswell, J. W. (2009) *Research Design: Qualitative, Quantitative, and Mixed Methods Approaches* (Thousand Oaks, CA: SAGE).

Denscombe, M. (2010) *The Good Research Guide*, 4th edn (Maidenhead: Open University Press).

Eggleston, J. and Klein, G. (1997) *Achieving Publication in Education*. Warwick Papers on Education Policy No. 7 (Stoke-on-Trent: Trentham Books).

Hart, E. (1996) Action research as a professionalising strategy: issues and dilemmas, *Journal of Advanced Nursing* 23: 454–461.

Kamler, B. and Thomson, P. (2006) *Helping Doctoral Students Write: Pedagogies for Supervision* (Abingdon: Routledge).

Kemmis, S. and McTaggart, R. (1990) *The Action Research Planner*, 3rd edn (Geelong, Victoria: Deakin University).

Major, C. H. and Savin-Baden, M. (2010) *An Introduction to Qualitative Research Synthesis: Managing the Information Explosion in Social Science Research* (Abingdon: Routledge).

Meyer, J. (2000) Using qualitative methods in health related action research, *British Medical Journal* 320: 178–181.

Meyer, J. and Land, R. (2003) *Threshold Concepts and Troublesome Knowledge: Linkages to Ways of Thinking and Practising within the Disciplines*. Occasional Report 4 (Edinburgh: Teaching, Learning and Research Programme, University of Edinburgh). Available at: http://www.etl.tla.ed.ac.uk//docs/ETLreport4.pdf.

Milgram, S. (1963) Behavioral study of obedience, *Journal of Abnormal and Social Psychology* 67(4): 371–378.

Newby, P. (2010) *Research Methods for Education* (Harlow: Pearson Education).

Opie, C. (2004) *Doing Educational Research: A Guide to First-Time Researchers* (London: SAGE).

Oxford University Press (2007) *Oxford English Dictionary* (Oxford: Oxford University Press).

Rowe, M. B. (1986) Wait time: slowing down may be a way of speeding up! *Journal of Teacher Education* 37: 43–50. Available at: http://studysites.sagepub.com/eis2study/articles/Budd%20Rowe.pdf.

Samaras, G., Bonoti, F. and Christidou, V. (2012) Exploring children's perceptions of scientists through drawings and interviews, *Procedia – Social and Behavioral Sciences* 46: 1541–1546.

Schon, D. (1983) *The Reflective Practitioner: How Professionals Think in Action* (New York: Basic Books).

Sikes, P. (2010) The ethics of writing life histories and narratives in educational research. In A. Bathmaker and P. Harnett (eds), *Exploring Learning, Identity and Power Through Life History and Narrative Research* (London: Routledge), pp. 11–24.

Smith, J. (2007) Life histories and career decisions of women teachers. PhD thesis, University of Leeds.

Thomas, G. (2009) *How To Do Your Research Project: A Guide for Students in Education and Applied Social Sciences* (London: SAGE).

Townsend, A. (2010) Action research. In D. Hartas (ed.), *Educational Research and Inquiry: Qualitative and Quantitative Approaches* (London: Continuum), pp. 131–144.

Townsend, A. (2012) *Action Research: The Challenges of Understanding and Changing Practice* (Maidenhead: Open University Press).

Wellington, J. J. (2000) *Educational Research: Contemporary Issues and Practical Approaches* (London: Continuum).

Whitehead, J. (2008) Using a living theory methodology in improving practice and generating educational knowledge in living theories, *Educational Journal of Living Theories* 1(1): 103–126.

Yin, R. K. (2009) *Case Study Research Design and Methods*, 4th edn (London: SAGE).

Index

A

action research 16, 55, 59, 63, 64–67, 69, 133–134
Adorno, Theodor 63
analysing data 27, 110
analysis bias 51
anonymity 15, 23, 53, 99, 102, 134

B

Becker (1986) 42
Boon (2014) 67

C

care 13, 20–21, 99
case studies 30, 31, 59, 72–74, 76, 88
confidentiality 15, 17, 53, 99, 102, 134
confirmation bias 50
control groups 21–22, 79, 108
Creswell (2009) 62
critical friendship 34
critical reading 33, 36
critical writing 33, 36, 41, 42
criticality 33–34, 74

D

data
    analysis software 123
    capture 85, 86, 102
    collection 26, 50–51, 64, 67, 69, 79, 80, 82, 85, 89–104
data, types of
    interval 111–112, 113
    nominal 92, 111–112, 113, 114
    ordinal 92, 93, 111–112, 113, 114
    ratio 93, 111–112, 113, 118
deception 19–20
descriptive statistics 70, 111–113, 114

design bias 51
Dewey, John 63
disciplinary perspectives 7
double-barrelled questions 94

E

ecological validity 79
Educational Endowment Foundation 76
Eggleston and Klein (1997) 47
epistemology 60, 62
ethics 13–14, 18, 21, 22, 29, 30, 52, 94, 98, 101, 102, 104, 134–135
ethics committee 24
ethnography 30, 101
experimental methodologies 76–79
external validity 108, 109

F

feminism 40, 41
Freire, Paulo 63

G

generalisability 69, 76, 87, 88, 108
Gove, Michael 29

H

harm 19, 20
    potential for 17, 18, 134
    protection from 14, 23
Hart (1996) 65
Hawthorne effect 79
honesty 4, 17–20, 29, 109
hypothesis 21, 69

I

informed consent 14, 15–16, 31, 70, 98, 101, 102, 134
internal validity 108, 109

interquartile range (IQR) 112, 113, 114, 117

interview 5, 15, 17, 20–21, 22, 23, 24, 26, 27–28, 51, 69, 73, 80, 81, 86, 96–99
  semi-structured 96
  structured 96
  transcripts 98, 109, 120, 121, 123–124, 135
  unstructured 96

K

Kamler and Thomson (2006) 34
Kemmis and McTaggart (1990) 64

L

Lalli (2015) 75
large-scale research 6, 55, 62, 76, 81
leading questions 26–27, 51, 56, 93–94, 98
Lee and Tsai (2010) 70
Lewin, Kurt 65
Likert scale 71

M

Major and Savin-Baden (2010) 109
Marx, Karl 41, 63
Marxist theory 39, 40, 41
matrix of themes 28, 37, 124
mean 112, 113, 117, 118, 119, 120
measure of dispersion 118
measures of central tendency 112, 113, 114, 118
median 112, 113, 114, 117, 118
meta-analysis 5, 109
methodology 5, 8, 40–41, 59, 64–67, 69, 71, 76, 101, 133–134
Meyer (2000) 65
Meyer and Land (2003) 8
Milgram, Stanley 19–20
mixed methods 63, 73, 79–81, 82
Mohamed (2014) 74

N

Newby (2010) 72

nonprobability sampling 86
  convenience 88
  purposive 88
  snowball 89

NVivo 123

O

observation 5, 22, 30, 75, 89, 99–102
  direct 73
  framework 134, 135
  participant 73, 101
  reactive 101
  structured 100
  unobtrusive 101
  unstructured 100
observational effect 108
ontology 8, 60–61
Opie (2004) 59

P

philosophy of research 59
Piggot-Irvine (2011) 81
praxis 65
probability sampling 86
  random stratified 87
  simple random 87
  systematic 87

Q

qualitative data 79, 80, 81, 82, 91, 120–125
qualitative framework 63, 75, 80, 81, 109
quantitative data 79, 80, 81, 82, 91, 100, 111–113
quantitative framework 63, 69, 109
question bias 51
questionnaires 26, 56, 57, 69, 80, 81, 90–95, 111, 113

R

randomised controlled trials (RCTs) 22, 76, 79
reflective practice 1, 74

reliability 107, 109–110

replication 108, 110

reporting findings 4, 5, 6, 17–18, 29, 52–53, 109–110, 133, 136

research as writing 34

research design 4, 8, 18–19, 20–21, 23–24, 25–26, 29, 55, 58, 73, 121

research literacy 8–10, 59

research protocol letter 15

research questions 25, 53

researcher bias 24, 26, 27, 29

researcher positionality 53

right to withdraw 15, 95

S

safeguarding 17

sampling 8, 51, 69, 85–89, 109

Scheiter, Schubert, Gerjets and Stalbovs (2015) 77

Schon, Donald 1

selection bias 51

self-protection 23

Sikes (2010) 24

small-scale research 6, 9, 22, 50, 52, 55, 90, 110, 120, 131–137

Smith (2007) 36, 40, 44, 125

standard deviation 70, 112, 113, 118–120

surveys 69–72

systematic investigation 3

T

thematic coding 27, 120–121, 123, 125, 135

theoretical framework 39–40, 70

Thomas (2009) 16, 24, 42

threshold concepts 8, 9

Townsend (2010) 65, 66

Townsend (2012) 65

V

validity 33, 38, 52, 53, 70, 72, 80, 86, 93, 99, 100, 107–110, 121

visual methods 22, 89, 102–104

W

Wellington (2000) 107

Whitehead (2008) 65

worldviews 38, 39–41, 60, 62–64
  participatory 63
  post-positivism 62
  pragmatic 63
  social constructivism 63

Y

Yin (2009) 73